THE SONGS OF HORSES

To Kristin,

Keep up the good work
it gets better and better —
all the time — it's great
watching your progress —
of course all the best

Paul

The Paul Belasik Trilogy

RIDING TOWARDS THE LIGHT – An Apprenticeship in the Art of Dressage Riding

EXPLORING DRESSAGE TECHNIQUES – Journeys into the Art of Classical Riding

THE SONGS OF HORSES – Seven Stories for Riding Teachers and Students

THE SONGS OF HORSES

Seven Stories for Riding Teachers and Students

PAUL BELASIK

J.A. ALLEN • LONDON

First published in Great Britain by
J.A. Allen
Clerkenwell House
45-47 Clerkenwell Green
London
EC1R 0HT
1999

British Library Cataloguing in Publication Data
A CIP record for this book is available from the British Library

ISBN 0 85131 7588

Editing, typesetting and layout by Lesley Gowers

Illustrations by Dianne Breeze

Printed in Hong Kong by
Dah Hua International Printing Press Co. Ltd

CONTENTS

I would like to dedicate this book to the poet A.R. Ammons, one of the greatest teachers from whom I have ever had the honour to learn something.

ACKNOWLEDGEMENTS

The quotation from *The Power and The Myth* by Joseph Cambell and Bill Moyers which appears in the Introduction is copyright © 1988 by Apostrophe S Productions, Inc. and Bill Moyers and Alfred Van der Marck Editions, Inc for itself and the estate of Joseph Campbell. Used by kind permission of Doubleday, a division of Random House Inc.

TEACHING RIDING: THE CIRCLE COMPLETES

For some thirty years, I have been studying the horse training systems of the world, past and present. This whole process, virtually from the beginning, has been well documented in a variety of media. I have published many articles and produced numerous audio and video tapes which have chronicled my progress, almost every step of the way. My books *Riding Towards the Light* and *Exploring Dressage Technique* are personal accounts of the process. Throughout, I have tried to be honest and to keep to my own experiences – I feel it is the only truly fair way to talk about these things. I hoped that the recordings might be a help or at least a comfort to others. Certainly they were to me.

Concurrently, silently, there was another education going on. It was just as serious, just as frightening, just as rewarding. It was every bit as difficult. It was my attempt to learn how to educate riders and to develop a system to teach riding. It involved many educational experiments. I received help and guidance from many special educators. The development was continuous, bouncing between research, study, experiment, and practice. It broke down into seven distinct phases or systems which covered a span of almost thirty years: from the most traditional of western teaching situations, being a college lecturer and conducting field and laboratory work, to very open alternative forms of education. From large groups to single individuals, from competitions to pure art, successes and failures.

Oddly enough, none of this process has ever been openly chronicled. No one person was with me long enough to know of its complete existence. I have never written about it nor even talked about it – until now. This book, the final one in the trilogy, is about that process. It is about teaching. It is not a book about what to teach: I have written plenty on that subject.

So, if this is not a book about what to teach, then, how do we teach? How do we learn? How do we know something?

First, how do we teach? Many of our lessons come from books. The study of dressage is no different. Many important lessons of the past masters have been documented. In my own education, I have relied heavily on codices like the books of Pluvinel and the Duke of Newcastle. However, it would be a great mistake to think this is how the bulk of teaching has been done. Most of the lessons of horsemanship have never been documented. To some scholars, the ancient Persians were the greatest horsemen who ever lived, but there are no volumes of Persian advice, no lists of their accomplishments. The amazing Islamic horsemen and the far eastern Russians have not written much either. Even the prestigious Spanish Riding School has few written directives.

So how is the bulk of horsemanship passed down? Through word of mouth, through myths, allegories and stories. For example, the mythological connections between humans and horses are rich and deep. Let me quote from the master mythologist Joseph Campbell when asked why anyone should care about myths:

'My first response would be "go on, live your life, it's a good life – you don't need mythology" ... One of our problems today is that we are not well acquainted with the literature of the spirit. We're interested in the news of the day and the problems of the hour. It used to be that the university campus was a kind of hermetically sealed-off area where the news of the day did not impinge upon your attention to the inner life and to the magnificent human heritage we have in our great tradition – Plato, Confucius, the Buddha, Goethe, and others who speak of the eternal values that have to do with the centring of our lives. When you get to be older, and the concerns of the day have all been attended to, and you turn to the inner life – well, if you don't know where it is or what it is, you'll be sorry.

'Greek and Latin and biblical literature used to be part of everyone's education. Now when these were dropped, a whole tradition of Occidental mythological information was lost. It used to be that these stories were in the minds of people. When the story is in your mind, then you see its relevance to something happening in your own life. It gives you perspective on what's happening to you. With the loss of that, we've really lost something because we don't have a comparable literature to take its place. These bits of information from ancient times, which have to do with the themes that have supported human life, built civilizations, and informed religions over the millennia, have to do with deep inner problems, inner mysteries, inner thresholds of passage, and if you don't know what the guide-signs are along the way, you have to work it out yourself. But once this subject catches you, there is such a feeling, from one or another of these traditions, of information of a deep, rich life-vivifying sort that you don't want to give it up.'

(Q: So we tell stories to come to terms with the world, to harmonise our lives with reality?
A: 'I think so, yes.')

So we have been taught by books, and stories, myths and allegories.

How do we learn? Current studies of the brain are just scratching the surface of the subject in terms of understanding the physiology behind learning. Researchers in education have gone far beyond the singular idea of intelligence as being testable in an hour's time with a pencil and paper. Howard Gardner, a professor of education and co-director of Project Zero at Harvard University, has developed a theory in use at hundreds of schools. This theory proposed that people possess different kinds of intelligence which can determine how each person learns. They have defined seven categories of intelligence: linguistic, musical, logical-mathematical, spatial, bodily-kinaesthetic, and inter- and intra-personal.

A truly gifted athlete, for example, may be at genius level in bodily-kinaesthetic awareness, but be more ordinary in linguistic skills. It is a mistake to assume bodily-kinaesthetic intelligence is somehow less intelligent or of less value than another form. The great Canadian ice-hockey player Wayne Gretzky said: 'Nine out of ten people think what I do is instinct. It isn't. Nobody would ever say a doctor had learned his profession by instinct: yet in my own way I've spent as much time studying hockey as a med student puts into studying medicine.'

If teachers teach in too mundane a manner they can miss a learner's real gifts, or special avenues of understanding. We learn in often very different ways. It is easy to see that learning and being taught are creative processes. It is important for teachers and schools to become aware of the vastly different ways in which people learn.

How do we know something? In my searching, I can think of no group of teachers as a whole who have tried more valiantly, or over a longer period of time, to get their students to experience knowledge than the Zen masters. They have tried in creative and sometimes seemingly bizarre ways to guide their students away from the trap of word knowledge into life experience, and the reality of the world of action.

Nuno Oliveira once made the statement that 'books are for people who already know how to ride'. When I heard this, I knew he was referring to the idea that the act of riding is primary. It is the reality. Books on riding can only augment action. They are relatively meaningless by themselves.

On the whole, and over the years, I have developed an affinity with and an admiration for other riding teachers. I see the best of them like Zen masters, driving themselves crazy to get their students to feel something, to do something, to experience something. I could not count how many times riders have asked me for exercises outside riding that they can do to help their riding. I used to concede some advice. Now I simply say that no, only riding will help your riding. Only eating will quell your hunger, only drinking will quench your thirst. Not only is riding the only thing that will help your riding, but it has to be a very specific kind of riding at that.

Campbell said that myths are 'the song of the universe, the music of spheres, that myths were metaphors for what lies behind the visible world .... However, the mystic traditions differ ... They are in accord in calling us to a deeper awareness of the very act of living itself.' The unpardonable sin, in Campbell's view, is the sin of

[13]

inadvertence, of not being alert, not quite awake.

I wrote *Riding Towards the Light* more than a decade ago; *Exploring Dressage Technique* followed a few years later. During thirty-odd years of riding, things have changed along the way. Once again, Campbell said it so well: 'The Indian yogi striving for release identifies himself with Light and never returns. But no one with a will to the service of others would permit himself such an escape. The ultimate aim of the quest must be neither release nor ecstasy for oneself but the wisdom and power to serve others.'

In my lectures over the years, I have noticed time and time again that when science-like material becomes too dry, and your audience is struggling, you can refresh them with a story. It is an ancient way to teach and to learn the most modern concepts.

So, here are some stories. For me, they are very important stories for they define my riding knowledge, and suggest ways to learn about riding as well as ways I have learned about riding. They are some of the ways I have been taught and perhaps they can suggest some ways to teach riding.

REFERENCES

CAMPBELL, JOSEPH WITH BILL MOYERS, *The Power of Myth*, Doubleday, New York, 1988.
GARDNER, HOWARD, *Frames of Mind: The Theory of Multiple Intelligences*, Basic Books, HarperCollins, 1983.

CHAPTER ONE

THE SYSTEM

Pennsylvania, 1997

A doctor friend of mine used to run a private training stable for disabled riders. One of her pupils, a young man in his twenties, had an incurable congenital condition of the soft tissue, which left his joints and muscles fused or contracted, in some cases non-existent. He weighed just seventy-eight pounds. Through his sheer courage, and some special teaching from my doctor friend, he had won several national awards. He had ridden for the United States at the World Dressage Disabled Championships in Denmark, and was now selected to represent his country again at the World Championships in England.

That particular year, my friend asked me if I would

work with this young man again to help prepare him for these championships. In disabled dressage championships, unlike those for the able-bodied, the rider does not bring his/her own horse. A horse is selected for each individual rider at each site, whether it be Stockholm, Lisbon, or, as in that particular year, London. There is just a very short time for acquaintance and preparation before the combinations are tested in the dressage arenas.

In my stable at that time, we had horses in training at all levels, from three-year-olds being broken to Grand Prix masters. We had but a short time to prepare. At first, my strategy was to help this young man to ride as many different horses as possible in the weeks prior to the championships. This would give him the widest range of experience so that he might be familiar with whatever type of horse he might draw in England.

So we began a series of lessons. My new student's condition had left him with little muscle mass, so, from the beginning, strength was a concern. Arthritis had severely constricted his hands so that normal dexterity and grip to hold the reins were impossible. Instead, my doctor friend had ingeniously rigged sets of wooden dowels which screwed into the reins, leaving a thick peg which my student could wedge between his bent fingers to prevent the reins from slipping. His fingers reminded me of the talons of one of my favourite hunting hawks, wrapping themselves around a wooden perch.

Although I respected such disabilities, I was not intimidated by them. In fact, I felt excited by the challenge of our work, especially by what I thought we could accomplish in our brief time together. However, I soon realised that there wasn't enough time to make complicated, substantive improvements in riding subtleties, which would take even a physically blessed athlete a long time to master.

As we went from horse to horse, an idea began to formulate. The one thing this rider *did* have was a fairly normal skeletal shape. I thought if I could somehow teach him to use his back, he could muster his minimal muscle power to stiffen or relax his body. I knew that this temporary rigidity could turn his body into a lever. I wanted most of all for him to feel how, if he held the reins and engaged his back, a horse could sink and tuck his croup under. Simultaneously the horse could extend and stretch his top line, thus firming up his spine in a big arch, ending with the poll up at the highest point – like a big wave swelling up and over. When the horse was balanced that way, the rider wouldn't need much strength to go into a different movement or make a change. If he could learn to set a horse up, then even if he had only small bursts of energy, these half-halts could re-balance a horse and set up turns or movements. If he ran into difficult horses, he could manoeuvre them without brute strength. If he could learn to use leverage on a horse, to adjust its balance, he could lighten it. He could learn to ride a horse with his bones!

We tried as many horses as I had access to, searching for a way to show him these feelings. However, I soon realised that there was only one horse in my stable that was completely trained to the back and seat, and was sensitive to the weight shifts I was trying to show this young man. This was my own Grand Prix horse who was 17 hands and in his prime, weighing 1450 pounds. He was, and still is, one of the strongest horses I have ever ridden in my life, and he was prone to humiliate riders by ignoring them, deliberately stiffening if they asked too harshly, seemed weak or over-reacted. When he was willing, he could collect all his mass and be as light as a deer.

On this particular day, I saddled this horse and took

him into the indoor riding hall. We started with some simple exercises but soon I felt I was near the same place in trying to explain subtleties of body control with the usual impotent phrases. Moreover, this time we were also strangled by severe time limitations.

If you do something for a long time and you try to practise well, you can become completely comfortable and familiar with your craft. Like a musician, you don't have to think about where exactly you will move your fingers. You just know that if you simply hold the instrument you can express a certain sound or feeling. I suppose that is similar to how I was feeling when I asked my student to stop my horse. Then I did something unusual. I am not sure why, because I had never done it before, but I decided to get up behind him on the horse. I had no idea how the horse would react to my additional weight, especially on his bare back behind the saddle. I didn't know if he would buck us both off. He had never been ridden double in his entire life! Even though I had never tried it before, I thought that if I could ask the horse in the right way, then maybe he would show my student what to look for, what to feel and then what to try. I had them both in front of me. Without any words to get in the way, we went off towards a place I knew so well.

I once calculated that by the time of this incident, I had ridden this horse over five thousand hours. Thus we were going on a very familiar journey – only I had never travelled with anyone else. Even in the countless hours of teaching lessons, the pupil heads off alone, flying solo. But here I was, sitting behind my pupil, like some flight instructor. The immediacy of the guidance and the relinquishing of control seemed strange. The connection, twin-like.

We began to work through some movements. Above

all, I wanted this young rider to feel how a horse could be collected so that he might be able to do it himself. His hands were in front of mine, his legs ahead of mine, his back in the saddle. Of course, I could not see his face, but people watching told me he wore an expression of enchantment as we worked. I could feel the horse doing just what I had hoped for. He moved forward with power but with a comfortable swing in his back. He made smooth, elastic transitions. Perhaps best of all, he settled and sank behind in the same tempo and rhythm. His whole front end seemed to grow up higher and higher in front of my student as the balance tipped back, and then forward again as we moved off. The horse showed him how a rider could control the horse's great strength and balance on command. I could feel when there were four hands on the reins, and when I let mine go to only my student's two. I could feel when I let my legs go, and my student kept riding him. Finally I could feel when I let go of my back, and horse and student were going by themselves.

I never really knew how my student felt, any more than you can know for certain how any person feels. Nor did I know how anyone watching felt. I could, however, feel when my student rode the horse, even if there were moments when he wasn't sure of what he was doing. I knew precisely when he was controlling this 1450-pound horse. It was a beautiful feeling. Those watching said it was a revelation.

When it was all done, I had some strong, but mixed feelings about the experience. I was very proud of my horse, but at the same time (although this might sound odd) I was not particularly proud of myself. I have never told many people about the experience.

To my mind, the incident was too theatrical. I didn't want to be that kind of teacher. I wanted my teaching to stand up to the scrutiny of the old European eye. I wondered how such a display would go down in the great schools I admired so much. How would those great old soldier-teachers react? I wanted to teach a system like theirs. I was unimpressed with my own flamboyance. I admired and respected the old soldiers, not because of some psychological need for their approval, but because I was keenly aware that my beloved dressage came to me because of their iron wills, their abhorrence of frivolity, their life-and-death attention and loyalty to the classical way. So I was not proud of that moment, even though I knew it was monumental. I decided that I would have to work towards a time when I could better understand why.

Thus I continued with my main preoccupation of searching for a system – a more universal approach for all students. And it was in this chasing that I eventually came upon my own enlightenment.

CHAPTER TWO

THE GRAND SILENCE

Somewhere in the countryside near Paris, 1735

It is ironic to say I had *heard* of his great horsemanship, since he was known as the Grand Silence. I had seen him hunting many times in the countryside near Paris, where I once had lived. I have to say that I thought of him then more as the Great Arrogance or the Great Pomposity. It was through the following twist of fate that I met him.

I was hunting an irascible goshawk in the woods not far from some open country where I knew he was hunting peregrine falcons with a member of the royal family. I had just come out of the thick cover when I heard the bells of a falcon. The bird was flying towards the forest carrying off a grouse. My first thought sprang from arrogance: I felt the Great Pomposity must be a better horseman than falconer. The bird was obviously too thin, and instead of staying with his kill until the falconers could retrieve him and the game, he had stolen off with it.

My smugness was to be short-lived. I let my attention falter for a moment and my own hawk, the larger bird of prey, bolted from my fist at the sight of the two-for-one. The peregrine, weighed down by his kill, was travelling slowly. Within seconds my bird struck the pair hard. Loose feathers swirled and floated free of the impact as the knot of birds hung still in the sky for a second before tumbling and cartwheeling toward the ground. When I got to the jumble, the peregrine's talons were locked into the grouse. The goshawk, by luck, had only her hallux (the thickest thumb-like talon) into the peregrine. It took me a whole half hour to sort them out. I kept thinking all the while that the Great Pomposity would ride down upon me and I would be finished. The peregrine must have come a long way with the small grouse because no one from the hunting party came near. No dogs, no horses. No one. The tension was stiffening my whole body. I covered the falcon with the silk scarf that I kept in my bag. I collected all the broken feathers. Under the dark of the silk he quieted and the cloth protected his plumage from further damage. My own hawk remained in a rage, her feathers raised, as I sorted her out from the middle of this scene of carnage. I returned to my horse and took the birds home.

In the days that followed I bathed the wound of the falcon and repaired fourteen broken feathers. I inserted fine wires into the hollow shafts of the feathers and, matching each piece as carefully as I could, I slid the straw-like shaft of the end onto the wire and cemented it with a special wax. Soon the bird would be able to fly well again instead of having to wait a whole year for a new moult.

The falcon ate well for me from the second day, and within two weeks I decided to return him to the Grand Silence.

I had no intention of riding down into his lair among the royalty at the great stables. At a nearby village, I found out where and when he was next hunting. Without knowing what to expect, I rode up to his party. I got close enough to see his face, and while I was giving some disembodied explanation, I was struck by what I saw. His intense, dark eyes were almost too big for his head. He had an inhuman stare, as if the skin around his eyes held his eyes in focus with a muscled grip. All expression in his face waited for orders from his eyes. He actually looked like a falcon.

I soon found that I had underestimated his reputation. He was far beyond arrogance. In order to be arrogant, one would have to entertain the idea of superiority or inferiority. His look suggested that the object of his gaze, namely me, was totally insignificant. I was beneath the realm of even ranking. At least that was how I felt when he looked at me.

When I left, one of his men came after me. He suggested that my riding needed help and if I wanted instruction, I could join Maitre's riding class at the manège of Monsieur Saumont. I thought then it was his way of thanking me.

That is how I started having riding lessons with the Grand Silence.

The first time I rode into the school and saw him out of his hunting clothes and in his riding attire, prepared to teach, he was an impressive sight. He wore a long sky-blue coat. It was tight across his chest, and had two long tails which were split like a swallow's tail lying behind him so as not to interfere with his seat. The coat was edged in golden trim. His wide sleeves were folded back elegantly to show a rich, red lining. Tucked into the wide sleeves were the gauntlets of his riding gloves. Those gloves were as long as a falconer's, but they were thin and soft and made from deerskin. They were the yellowy colour of butter. He wore a three-cornered hat. His long boots were made of supple, thick, dark leather, and they rose well over his knees.

When he rode, it was a revelation. He was the consummate athlete, artist, dancer. Over the roughest ground his great legs kept him steady. In the school, he was all grace, power and delicacy. His students learned by imitation because, above all, he was silent. He was insistent, though, that we learn with our hearts, not just with our eyes.

Someone once suggested that the lessons at Monsieur Saumont's were not on the same level as those when Maitre was working near the palace. I found out this was not so. He was totally incapable of changing his working style. There was not a duplicitous bone in his whole body. He had only one standard for riding, and it was the highest flag on the pole.

It was difficult to know what he was watching for in the practices because he frequently rode in the classes, training one horse or another. He would often stop and watch a single rider and then ride on again. It became painfully obvious to us all, at one time or another, that there was no hope in trying to guess what he wanted to see, or of pleasing him, especially if under his eyes you lost your attention in your own work or your problem at hand. If such a thing happened, he would immediately pick up the reins and ride on. The first steps of his wordless ride would be the equivalent of a screaming exclamation or a mere muttering. No matter where he was positioned in the school, he would turn away from you, and when his eyes broke from you, it seemed there was a perceptible cracking sound. Invariably, he would then execute some of his most brilliant riding. It was as if only the highest form of riding could purify the air from the stench of this ungodly mediocrity, created by these impossible students.

Anyone who thought a pirouette was a pirouette was a pirouette never felt or saw the Maitre turn away from an aggravating student. His turns could convey every minute degree of emotion. His horse might simply revolve in a walk, and effortlessly engage into a trot or a canter. That might mean mild approval. His horse might also turn on the deepest set haunches, fast, high in front, exploding into a caprioling kind of canter – a turn that could not be executed quickly enough to rid his eyes of a most revolting sight of some grovelling pupil. As long as you yourself weren't the object of his silent comments, these incidents were fascinating to watch.

I think he must have hated words; and if he did, he especially hated words that suggested limitation, and he reserved his greatest disgust for the word 'impossible'. The last thing you ever wanted to do, no matter how much trouble you might be in during a movement or practice, was to suggest that the movement was impossible, or worse, that the horse was incapable of it. For he would then ride your horse, in front of you and whoever else might be in the school at the time. He would begin to work on your problem and always he would fix it. It would happen so smoothly, so seemingly effortlessly, so quickly and with such ease. The more he got the impression you thought something was impossible, the greater the ease with which he finished off your tiny protests. At these moments, you didn't know what to do. You would at once wallow in your own self-pity, feeling hopeless, realising the size of the gulf between your own skill and his, and also be mesmerised with inspiration by his incredible gifts.

Sometimes certain students would be wise to the fact that he would ride their problems away if they looked confused. To whine for his attention was a very big gamble. It was almost always a big mistake as he had unbelievable peripheral perception and he would be in the middle of some cyclone of problems when his eye would catch you resting or in a bad position. He was always aware if you were having trouble. Some of us came to realise that it was a compliment if he let you struggle, as long as your struggle didn't demean the horse. On the other hand, if he once categorised you as a slacker, he would patronise you imperceptibly and the course of your instruction would never be of the same standard again. It was practically, if not totally, impossible to break out of this category once you walked yourself into it. I think he took it as a personal insult. It was as if he wasn't a good enough horseman to know what you and your horse were capable of.

Of all the horses he rode, one really stuck out. The great Florido. Florido was a Spanish stallion – white with a translucent softness of marble. There was a glassine quality to his coat, and in different light it could refract like prisms, making him look blue. He was average in size, with a thick mane and tail. He was feline in his disposition. He was at times quiet, almost lazy, and when he intended action, he could be so fast you had to remember his movement. What was most amazing was his almost human intelligence. Together they were a team. It seemed that only on a horse like Florido could the Grand Silence use up all his skill.

Oddly, it was an incident that had nothing to do with their riding together that showed me how connected they were. One of the royal nephews had attempted a courbette on a young stallion. The inexperienced horse bolted with the even more inexperienced rider. In a moment the horse was at full speed rounding the short end of the school. The Grand Silence and Florido were working at the other end. In less than a second, the man slowed Florido and without stopping, he swung his outside leg high over the sinking haunches of his horse. The tails of his blue coat were caught by his leg as he spun in a dismount, stepping from his other stirrup to the ground. The blue coat spread out in a cool blue fan above the blue horse. In the same motion, his gloved hand dropped the reins on top of the neck of Florido. Then, as if in a perfectly choreographed dance, they stepped away from each other. The Grand Silence strode without running, without a word, slicing the distance, cutting off his prey. As the young stallion rounded the corner and began to gallop down the long wall, the Grand Silence was there. Florido stepped in the other direction until man and horse were positioned almost exactly opposite one another on either side of the manège. The Grand Silence stood still, his legs slightly spread, his hands resting at his sides. Florido nickered. It was odd: the man silent, the horse talking.

When the young stallion made the turn heading toward the Grand Silence, it had a choice. Long before it had to face the Grand Silence, it veered away, and ran toward Florido. Then it began to circle Florido as if it were being lunged by the older stallion. Florido nickered again, and the young stallion stopped and carefully approached him, arching his neck like a cautious swan. He never noticed the Grand Silence approaching. Just before the young stallion was about to touch noses with Florido, the gloved hand of the Grand Silence closed its fingers around the rein and held it tight. The gloved fist

[27]

was raised in the air. Quiet and strong, the way it is offered as a perch for a falcon. The stallion was subdued. It was as if the Grand Silence would never let this impudent renegade actually touch the great Spanish horse.

* * * * *

There was a ride performed by the Grand Silence on Florido which comes to mind as the greatest sustained piece of riding I have ever seen. It is something that I do not say lightly because I have seen some exquisite pieces of horsemanship which may have equalled this event in brilliance or ingenuity, style or power. But there was no equal to that ride as a complete moment. The evening I saw that ride was the first time in my life that I saw a man alter linear time. The man and his horse defeated the science of his day. They went beyond time. No one that I talked to afterwards, even months later, could remember just how long in time this event had taken. Was it an hour? Half an hour? No one took their eyes off man or horse until the Grand Silence and Florido stopped.

This demonstration ride was to take place at a royal party, an occasion which was to feature a heavy equestrian flavour. There was the usual list of socialite guests, but there were also quite a few noted horseman and women. As his riders, the Grand Silence expected us all to work. For all intents and purposes we were, in addition to our riding duties, to serve as waiters for the cognoscenti. It was important to the Grand Silence that the horse people were looked after properly.

The longer I had been around him, the more I admired him. However, I could never understand how he functioned in such a strangling political atmosphere. Was he so socially crafty? How, without words, did he stay ahead of a seemingly million jealous *écuyers*? Maybe he hunted so much and rode so much to stay out of the suffocating tent of gossip and intrigue. He must have had skills outside his riding that we never saw. (Of course, he had political skills we never saw – he had subtle riding skills we never saw!) He seemed indefatigable and yet I wondered what a toll all of this was taking internally. Maybe the brilliance of his riding was the release. One never knew. He was not easy to figure out. Looking back on that evening, I have always felt that the cause behind what turned out to be brilliance but at first seemed like disaster, was sparked by stupidity or jealousy. In that high atmosphere a prank can seem like sedition. I later found out that was how it was treated.

The gala evening had been proceeding as a great success. There were hundreds and hundreds of guests, and several performances of the quadrille. Part of the evening's programme was a solo ride by Maitre on Florido, accompanied by a musical arrangement. The musicians were situated across the riding area, facing the guests, so as to achieve the best acoustics since they were some distance from their audience. I knew this ride would be near perfection. I also knew that Maitre would not upstage anyone, so I was sure the performance would be gracious and short.

Somehow, though I never found out how, the music stopped in the middle of his ride. There seemed to be considerable confusion. I swear I could see the hawk glare of his eyes from where I was near the wall. As can happen with crowds, their collective rhythm stopped, murmurs of conversation quieted, glasses stopped tinkling and faces seemed to wince in irritation. I am sure he felt some embarrassment that the party might lose its ambiance.

Then, from the middle of the hall, he began a passage with Florido that was so exquisite in its cadence that it brought smiles back to the guests. He continued, however, to escalate the rhythm and the height of the steps until the people's expressions clearly changed to amazement. He did not stop and the passage became even higher. It became so high and so cadenced it almost began to frighten some of the guests because it looked as if he were about to leave the ground. There were many members of the audience who could not handle the tension. They did not know what might happen to their minds if he *did* leave the ground. It was all so surreal.

I don't know if Florido was so excited that his coat began to glisten with moisture, but it was as if a beam of moonlight had fixated on him, turning his coat into vibrant silver.

The passage was drum-like. Some of the Spanish men stood up taller, as if about to break into a dance. The Maitre then settled the passage down and, in turn, brought it closer to one group of people after another. There he placed the great horse in a piaffe and raised it to brilliance before moving on. He turned the passage, curved it, circled it, changed its rhythm and intensity. He let the people almost feel the horse. Without one musical note, he began his own concert of motion.

Just when the guests were almost drunk with his powerful cadences and hard lines, he would drop into delicate side-passes and voltes. This amazed me. I knew him as a hunter, as the man's man. Yet he and the stallion moved with as much freshness and femininity as a week-old filly. From there, Maitre went off into gallops so fast and powerful that the audience backed away from the riding area. It was astounding on so many levels.

This remarkable ride was completely commanding yet not at all boastful. I knew he hated showing off. Many times during practices, if someone held a horse in levade too long, the old *écuyers,* who were his lieutenants, would quickly intervene in an effort to shield the student from the Grand Silence. They knew if he saw such a demonstration, the rebuke would be severe. 'Did you think the old *écuyers* were going blind? Did you think we needed to see you work a little longer? Perhaps the old men are going deaf so your riding should shout at them!' The old *écuyers* would remind the riders that humility and modesty of movement showed reverence for your horse. Knowledgeable horsemen could see good work without excessive trappings and flair. Flamboyance has no place among true riders.

The Grand Silence continued to move, it seemed, without effort. He was inventing new movements and patterns that none of us had ever seen before. Sometimes the man and the horse were as a war chant, sometimes a love song. It seemed he was taking movement to such a high form that it trivialised the music that was absent. It is hard to believe but I think that was what he was doing. With silent passion, he was excited by his own anger, but he controlled it. He burned it up like a fuel for his actions. Wherever the ferocity of his energy came from, he somehow got the horse to find it too. Then he married them until there was a motion unlike anything either a man or a horse would be capable of on their own. For good measure, maybe obsessive control or perhaps the pure love of art, he controlled the flame. This flame was the sound, the tempo, the rhythm, the visual juxtapositions. He had taken the simple idea of moving in space on a flat plane from one place to another, and turned motion into emotion. He could make you feel what he was trying to show. This process, this manipulation, of space in space, was his art.

That night, when the music stopped, he was forced to stand up his art and let everyone who wished, see it – naked, amoral, brilliant.

And when he stopped the stallion before the king and saluted, the place went crazy. The party exploded with cheers. I watched him intensely as he accepted the bravos, then politely and tactfully made his way back toward a couple of his lieutenants. I forced my way through the crowd. I wanted to see him closer, to see and hear what he might say to the people.

I got near and heard one of his trusted aides say to him, 'That was some exhibition!' He looked at his aide with a stern face and said, 'That was not an exhibition. I am not an exhibitionist. That was a lesson.'

During the next week, I saw more parts of that lesson, for it was not over. Several familiar faces close to him were no longer to be seen. If he could not trust someone, the cut was made quickly and sharply.

As time went on, and I went travelling, I would often hear the strangest remarks about him. I heard people say that he ran the bloodiest manege in all of France. It was the stupidest, most ignorant of criticisms. He never struck a confused horse or rider. It was not necessary. Wilful riders appeared, but none were a match for his technique and skills. He could dispense with them almost effortlessly. The longer I knew him, the more the force of his character grew, and I saw the gifts of his reflexes from softness to firmness get better and better. Yet there were so many fools who would watch and try to imitate him and his riding without any apparent regard for its difficulty, so some self- destructed. He wasn't going to stop them. Neither would he defend or explain himself. His riding would speak for him. Those who were too ignorant or arrogant to know what he was about, what he was doing, were just that. And he would not tell them otherwise.

I also began to long for some explanation of what he did and when and why. All one ever heard about was his great strength. But I knew enough to know that he was not about riding with strength. How did he know how to shift his intentions? What told him? Why did he pick one course of action over another? How could I learn to understand his vocabulary of motion?

This yearning would not subside. I felt I had to search somewhere else. Feeling like a traitor, I left France and went away from him.

I had already found my own lord.

CHAPTER THREE

THE COUNT
Belgium, 1890

The Doctor was one of the best conversationalists I had ever met. He seemed to know every equestrian personality in Europe. Since his retirement, his competitiveness and rivalries with them had subsided so they were very friendly to him. His guidance was invaluable to me.

We had a silent kind of deal, the Doctor and I. When I was in need of his counsel, I would make a pilgrimage to his home in a small village in the south of Belgium. I would always ask if I could take him to dinner, and each time he would select the same old hotel. To get there we would hire a carriage and travel on a road that cut in and out of a high pine forest. The trees grew right down to the edge of a boulder-strewn river that gave the road its direction. In winter the trip could be unpleasant because the moisture in the valley produced a coldness that could penetrate the heaviest coat or lap robes. Yet it was those winter trips that made the old hotel even more hospitable. Once a castle, the hotel was positioned on the highest ground, which made it look like a small Tibetan monastery.

The hotel was small by grand standards, but it had great charm. The inside was almost entirely finished in oak panels with high walls and sweeping curved and moulded ceilings. Yet the dining rooms were broken off in smaller sizes with burning fireplaces of natural stone in the winter and wide, long, open windows in the summer. You could look straight out into the air above the river valley. The rooms made you feel comfortable and private. We had some special meals there.

This time I wanted to know about a Hungarian Count. People had said that in the old days, the Doctor and the Count were great friends, like brothers, before their families and duties took them in different directions. I knew enough not to ask him for these dossiers right off or he could start on one of his usual tirades of how they were all charlatans and so on. So I waited. We had some wine, and later a brandy or two. Then I felt I could ask him anything. So I brought up the subject of the Count. His lips cracked in a sarcastic but benevolent smile. I told him I felt I needed to work with someone who could ride well, but who also had a real intellectual understanding of riding and training and took that kind of approach. The Count's equestrian writings were encyclopaedic and it was well known that he could also ride. I thought he would be the perfect choice to further my learning of how to ride and teach.

'He is an intellectual,' the Doctor agreed. 'Perhaps one of the most intelligent horseman that has ever lived.'

'He is a scientist,' he continued. This was actually very high praise from the Doctor. 'However,' he said, 'he can be deceitful and political. He is a very clever man. Someday I will tell you about that side of him. If you still insist on going, I will supply you with an introduction.'

It all seemed to go so easily for me. The topic shifted and we shared some very funny stories. When we were about to leave, he stopped. 'There is one thing you need to know about the Count: in spite of his brilliance, which is genuine, horses are not his first love...' I must have looked surprised. He continued. '...women are. Being a young man, you may find it difficult to get his attention.'

I was not unattractive when I was young, and soon after I arrived with my introduction from the Doctor, I was afraid the women there would put too much tension in the air. I couldn't help feeling as if I was some sort of replacement possibility for the young women, who thought of the Count as a grandfather, and the older ones, who were tired of his seductions. However, instead of being jealous, he was amused by all the intrigue and distractions. As always, he was fascinated by women's reactions, especially to different men. It was another chance for him to study women. When his young female assistant, who was also his secretary, and I promptly fell in love, all the workings of the inner sanctum were open to me. She and the Count were very close, and he was captivated with our trying to carry on a love affair and getting all our work done besides.

The Count's stable was in a fairly remote village near the border with Germany. It was an elegantly simple arrangement of stone buildings. The stables, his office, the riding hall, his home, the guest quarters and dormitory were all situated around a cobblestone courtyard. His long office was on the second floor above a section of stables. From there he knew all the comings and goings of guests and students, business or entertainment.

On many evenings, his office lamp, whose light glowed yellow on the irregular stones of the yard, was the last to go out. It was there he kept his library, and did his writing. It was similar to a sculptor's studio, large and spacious, with models of human skeletons and many large bleached bones from horses. It was also like a scientist's laboratory, with mechanical levels and a draftsman's drawing table. At one end was his desk, which always seemed to be covered with opened books and papers except for the small area where he wrote. There were shelves of his beloved books in every language. He spoke and could read five languages. The Count challenged even the most simple assumptions. He was forever measuring everything. He always carried a little measuring tape, like the cloth one of a seamstress, but one that reeled into a tiny canister like a miniature fly-fishing reel. It looked like a silver locket. His over-developed sense of noblesse oblige could tolerate the ignorance of almost any class of students, but nothing could hide his dislike for stupid people, especially stupid men. So we all had to study. But I felt I had to study harder, and I loved it.

Lunchtime at his school was a communal affair where he often expounded on his latest theories or explanations of the day's work or problems. These times were not always the best situations for digestion. He could be combative and testing, and he adored it if you could joust with him. You just had to be careful that you stayed with what you knew or else kept it in question form. If you over-stepped the mark, or were a touch arrogant, you were in trouble. He was too well read, too good a speaker and too cunning. Intellectually he was indomitable, and on the subject of horse, practically divine.

One of the things I liked most about him was his passion for learning, which even he didn't seem to be able to control, and which could be triggered by anything. It was difficult to speculate on all of his motives. However, if, at one of the lunches, something caught his attention, a different application of theory or a question which he couldn't immediately answer, you could see his interest light up. On those occasions his office lamp would be burning deep into the night.

While we were resting or out at some inn, he was moving farther, deeper and deeper into the darkness of his exploration. It seemed to me that no one could ever catch up with him. He was so far ahead. He just could not bear not to understand how something worked, or what someone meant in their writings. He had read so much that it seemed as if he could talk to deceased writers! And doing so, he could draw explanations from ambiguous texts or have clear insight into a vague statement. After he had worked for days or months on a problem, as soon as it was clear, he would write it up. Or he would tell us in us perfectly edited little speech what he had found. He was not in any way selfish with his knowledge. Even if he were critical, I found it hard to dislike him. I always felt grateful.

Not long after I arrived there, a wealthy young couple who had a horse in training with the Count, came out from the city to spend a couple of days and watch their horse's progress. Very shortly after they arrived, they came down to the stables. I think they had no idea the Count's assistant would be a young woman. Before the Count came out they began to treat the assistant in a very condescending way. I wanted to defend her, but I was too new and unless she asked for something, I had to defer to her authority in matters of the stable. I felt helpless, and just as their arrogance reached an unbearable limit, the Count appeared. He instantly assessed the situation.

They had made two mistakes. The first was they didn't know how the Count felt about women. The second was that this particular woman had been with him since she was a young girl, and he thought of her as a difficult daughter, which to him was even more endearing than a well-behaved one. The kind of superiority they displayed had the patronising property of speaking with veiled gentility. It is usually best revealed in language. It can be revealed in dress or action, but without words, this could just be eccentricity. In their case the thickness of the veil was irrelevant because there was no gentility behind it. These people forgot that position is something that is bestowed from a collective consensus. It is done to you. You cannot do it to yourself. It is not the state of an individual's mind. It is more the state of the state's mind. And in this particular little state, the Count's school, the Count was the absolute governor.

Their horse was prepared to be ridden. It was brought out for the Count to ride. He didn't move. Instead, nonchalantly, he informed them that his assistant would ride it. There was a palpable indignation, and silence. A real chess game of innuendo and suggestion began. But the Count would not budge. He just kept talking. They must have thought he was the stupidest man on the earth. No matter how increasingly blatant their opinions became or how lightly disguised their criticisms, he increasingly and completely ignored them. Or worse, when he could sense they were about to say something else, he would start first with counter praise that began to shake their security. The Count had no temper. When you coupled this coolness with his rapier intelligence, he could be verbally devastating. The next day the couple made an excuse and left early.

The school was often visited by owners, and the Count had a way of weeding out the time-wasters. In some cases, when he was courting someone's patronage, he would suffer fools unmercifully. On the other hand, if someone crossed his sense of independence, no matter how much he may have needed the business, they were dismissed, and there was no pardon. After that incident, I have to admit I became a loyal subject.

One of the Count's special talents was his photographic memory. Often, when we were riding in a lesson or practice and he noticed something, he would have you ride the movement over and over as if he were making a series of sequential mental paintings. Then, when he had the entire problem mapped, if the solution was not obvious, he would be able to take his pictures and study the horse or problem at will. Sooner or later he would have an answer or an explanation.

In all the time I spent there I never saw him so excited as when he was working on his famous paper, 'Sympathetic Responses in Horses and Humans'. I was fortunate enough to witness the development of the whole project. I watched him take an idea, test it through theory, and then actually put it into reality. Maybe he was excited because he honestly felt that this particular work was his most important. For him, and others, it became a proof of collection of the horse and a proof of how his forward riding method was the best way to achieve collection. After he wrote this treatise his teaching changed and this work became one of the consistent threads throughout his teachings. In any case I definitely remember exactly where his inspiration came from for this involved piece of research.

The Count had been on holiday in Scandinavia with some of his friends, one of whom was an oceanographer. They had ventured out into the North Sea, where they watched many whales swimming and breaching. The Count was familiar with all the current research on locomotion but there was something fascinating about the particular way in which the whales breached. He was intrigued by the amount of power they could generate to raise their gigantic bodies high out of the water.

When he came back he kept saying that he'd seen whales doing airs above the sea! And that whales could do the best levades and courbettes. That, after all, is exactly what he saw. In the generation of their power they moved their great flukes like horses move their hind legs. Where horses curled their hips under, flexed and pushed off the ground, these great cetaceans brought their flukes under them, and then with a tremendous push against the semi-solid sea water, they came up vertically. He told us how he had asked his friend if any other fish moved like that. His friend told him essentially not. Then he asked his friend if this horizontal fluke movement was a sea-mammal trait. The scientist told him yes, and then reminded him that the mammals of the sea first evolved on land and later moved to the sea. He said that there were still residual small appendages on some whales' pelvises. They were relics from a long time ago when they had legs and moved on land. It was that exchange, the Count later said, that inspired a startling revelation.

One day, soon after his return, we were all at lunch and he brought his small human skeleton to the table. We knew he had been working on something new and pretty important. So we all sat alert. He took the skeleton in his hand and tipped it over so that it was in the position of a person crawling. He looked up at us all half smiling, half very serious. Then, in his challenging teacher's voice, asked, 'What is this?'

I think we all felt trapped, and none of us ventured anything. He waited a little longer than usual for the answer. 'Ah,' he said mocking us. 'You are so young and already you have lost your imaginations. It is a horse!' he exclaimed.

I found it was at times like this that one had to be very fast to keep up with him. The worse thing you could do would be to blurt out a stupid answer, just to relieve the pressure of the silence. That would usually throw him off the rhythm of his little theatre and earn you a sarcastic comment. If instead, you waited and listened, and kept looking at him like you were thinking and almost getting it, concentrating, listening, he would sense your confusion and come around again in another way. If you could bear the pressure of waiting, with each of his passes and explanations, his look of exasperation would get tempered by his fatherly patience. His face seemed to strain under his crushing duty.

If you could stand it, you would get it. He would not give up until he could articulate his idea clearly enough for you to understand. I am not talking about waiting a few minutes. I am talking about sometimes waiting for days before he could find a way, struggling with some of the more subtle or complex riding issues.

That particular day he began to explain things to us by asking: if he put up the skeletal structure of a horse, the skeletal structure of a human and the analogous defining structure of a cockroach, which two would be most similar? Then he asked about a whale, a human, and a snake, and which would be the most different.

He told us how at first he was simply attracted by the whale's movement and the horse's movement. But upon some investigation he realised that the similarity of movement was governed by the similarity of anatomical structure. At first this resonance seemed bizarre because the animals moved in such different mediums. But when his friend pointed out the animals' common evolutionary mammalian past he realised how strong these roots were. The laws of motion were so intrinsic in the bodies of mammals that they were even stronger than the mediums of sea or land. They were stronger than the pressure of any place they might end up. He extrapolated that the same similarities must exist between a horse and a man.

Would that not help explain so many of those mysterious riding position connections? The rider extends his spine, brings his chin in, arches his extended neck, and the horse does the same. This rider's position puts the horse on the bit by teaching the horse through a sympathetic gesture. The horse can easily relate because it has an almost identical underlying anatomical nervous and skeletal structure. If the rider projects the centre of gravity forward, the horse, imitating, moves forward.

In the next days during our riding lessons, we uncovered hundreds of these gestures. Then he showed us a vivid example of how unknowingly this same power backfires in an unintellectual or unsympathetic rider. Sympathetic gestures can be complex, he explained, and they can at the same time work in concert with each other. Or they can be antagonistic. He felt that most riders, whether they know it or not, were often training unconsciously with these gestures.

Then, there is the uneducated rider who tries to drive the horse with his seat bones. This rider curls his hips under, rounding his back, thereby sitting further back on his buttocks and pushing hard down and apparently under. The rider's intention is for the horse to follow – tuck its hips under, sit a little more on the haunches and collect or engage. But the horse does not follow this. So the rider tries harder. The harder he tries, the more he depresses the back of the horse and the horse locks his hind legs out behind. The horse's pelvis tips the opposite way to the rider's intention. The Count said any thinking rider should have been able to figure out why this kind of seat was oppressive and impossible. That even though the sympathetic gestures resonate from a common evolutionary part, different orientations developed over time.

The whale, so similar to the horse, became oriented to the sea and now cannot walk on the land, The horse on the other hand is a quadruped and developed a horizontal orientation towards the effects of gravity. Man developed a vertical orientation. 'You see,' he said, 'it's almost as though the brain is older than the bodies they command. The brain, the memory of common ancestry, is very strong, but things changed. One quadruped moves to the sea and becomes a swimmer. One quadruped remains on land and becomes a great runner. One quadruped remains on land and learns to walk upright, becoming bipedal. The unthinking rider reacts reflexively from common and prehistoric memory. This memory now becomes non-functional. The whale can't walk on land, yet it might remember it in its body's core.' It was his opinion that, as far as he knew, only the THINKING man, of all these animals, could circumvent orientation – and he could do this with his imagination.

The intelligent rider/trainer's greatest attribute is not his body or talent which can be stuck in an orientation whether it be vertical, horizontal or in another certain medium. Rather, it is the rider's mind and therefore the freedom gained from the powers of this imagining tool.

When the Count showed us that human skeleton, tipped over crawling, and asked us to imagine that it was a horse, he was showing us how we could design ways to solve riding problems by trying to understand the complexities of sympathetic gestures. Crude riders are often running into walls because, whether they know it or not, their riding is being controlled by the prehistoric evolution of their bodies. This works a lot of the time because there are a great many evolutionary similarities in mammals. However, there are limitations that have to be addressed outside the physical plane.

The crude rider tirelessly shows the horse how to tip its pelvis, to collect over and over, not realising the horse can't follow the imitation because it is a quadruped with the opposite gravitational alignment. Now if the rider is crude enough, he will persist with so much force, that the horse may try anything to relieve the oppression, in spite of the rider. The thinking rider changes his vertical orientation in his mind to a horizontal one and can invent a way to work in the orientation of the horse, even though it is not his own orientation. In fact, the thinking rider can solve the problem by education with a sympathetic gesture, but a different one. When the rider tips the seat way under, he breaks at the waist. The rider immediately loses the firmness of the elongated spinal line. His body is as useless as a broken lever, no matter how hard he pushes. The truly collected or collectable horse does not imitate just the pelvic tip. It imitates the firm extended spine of a rider in a good position. Once they are sympathetically aligned in firmness, the rider, with the slightest leverage backwards, shows the horse to lower its haunches not lower its back. Sympathetic gestures could be very complex and even contradictory, but they could be revealing and educating as well.

The Count did not want us to get stuck in believing this theory was some kind of game with a certain key for every lock. Most of all he was telling us to use our imagination and minds to step out of the limiting boundaries of our own physical bodies. The freedom in itself could be intoxicating, but it could also yield useful practical results.

This work had a huge effect on me. It was explosively emancipating. On a physical level it clarified so many loose ends for me. It was clear why collection had to come after strong forward riding. Connection, that is firmness, had to come before leverage was possible. If not, you could easily hollow the horse's back and actually force it to evade and be crooked. It all seemed so logical. I realised more than ever how important rider-position was. I saw how lifting the chest of the rider, for example, could lift the chest of the horse. Above all, I felt I really locked on to his message about using one's imagination, using the mind to help the body. I felt I was learning how to learn, and because of that I was learning more about riding than at any time in my life. Some of us felt like we were on top of the whole equestrian world in our little enclave.

* * * * *

Because the farm was remote, the Count's equestrian friends usually stayed in his guest house for a few days whenever they came to visit. These were always festive times with beautiful dinners, and often we were all invited. Always there was the most stimulating conversation. Although he would never admit it, the Count loved gossip and would get excited when his guests updated him on all the equestrian happenings in their parts of the world. Most of his talk would turn up disparaging information about one or another horseman's knowledge or skill. He never minded hearing about a certain horseman's lack of skill, but if he heard about brutality or cruelty this finished off the horseman in his eyes, immediately and forever. And he never forgot them. All in all, I think he was secretly wanting to hear about when and where someone had seen a great horseman. If this did happen he made the visitor carefully recount every detail. It would not take him long, usually a year, before he would somehow make a journey to meet this rider and see the phenomenon for himself. We were so fortunate to hear his first-hand views and opinions of some of the greatest horsemen he had come to know.

Monsieur Etienne Noble, the Count's French friend and a trainer, arranged to visit for a few days. He had unfortunate timing, for the Count was so fresh from his recent discoveries, that it seemed every theoretical point made by Noble could be crushed by the Count's latest thinking. When Noble rode, he had a habit of pricking the horse in the stomach with his spur points. It was his belief that this would lift the back of the horse as the abdominal muscles reacted to the spurs. The Count told him he thought the practice was worthless as an exercise. It was simply a reflex and one could never sustain the position through a whole riding session. He asked how Noble was going to regulate the size or speed of the response if it were mere reflex. He seemed particularly harsh and I was sure he hurt Noble's feelings.

Over the course of two days he systematically presented everything he had found out or been thinking to Noble. When the time came for Noble to leave, they seemed on the best of terms. Certainly Noble did not leave disturbed. After Noble had left, one of the students inadvertently suggested that Noble was stupid. The Count got very sharp. He said Noble had never been stupid. He was ignorant of the new work, and that was the reason the Count argued with him. It was to present his best case to Noble as a matter of honour. It would have been disrespectful to present anything less. He told us one of the reasons they became friends was because, at one time, the Count had been ignorant about Spanish horses. It was Noble who generously taught him all about them.

Through situations like that, the Count continued to grow in my eyes. Coupled with my own romantic endeavours, it was one of the reasons I stayed with him longer than with any other teacher or trainer. I think, though, that this infatuation with his great intellect was also why I failed to see, or failed to want to see, something which may sound strange, but which I came to realise was unfortunately true. The horses at his stable were not progressing in their training. Even horses in training a year or more showed little improvement. He seemed constantly to give up on the physical problems. His famous 'enough for today' became not a slogan of his great patience, as much as an excuse for not pressing with the work if it got too difficult. Whilst he was trying to teach us to move with our imaginations outside the limits of our physical bodies to solve problems, he would often stop there. If he shifted something mentally, corrected a problem, he didn't always feel the need to correct it physically. It almost lost its appeal. This became difficult to ignore the longer I stayed.

It was almost beside the point, but if you added this to what would happen if a beautiful woman came around, almost all substantial work could come to a standstill.

Toward the end of my time with the Count, his assistant and I had fallen out of love and I was feeling edgy, ready for a change. I remember we were all helping the Count prepare for a rather large party he was giving. At one point when everything seemed prepared he sat us all down with some sherry before the guests arrived. I thought he would hold court in his usual fatherly style but he seemed a little softer, more human. He said, 'You will find that five people may know something and then five hundred will read about or hear about it and they will be the type that feel they know it also. Now you may come along and it will look like five hundred and five people know the answer to your inquiry. If you begin asking at random the odds of your finding the one who really knows the answer are very slim. It would be possible for you to go off in hundreds of false starts, blind alleys. It is very possible that in a lifetime with a time limit you could simply make the wrong choices and go through your whole life without ever getting to the one who might hold the answer for you. The one who could truly help you. You have to find a way to cut down those odds. To be able to see through people, or personalities, or situations, faster, more intuitively. Gauge them from a different place inside yourself, use more than just your mind. Above all, don't let the opinions of society or reputation prejudice your own experience.'

Sometimes you hear a public statement that resonates with your mood so strongly you feel the statement was made for you. I thought that. I knew he was right and saw it as the way to find one's teachers. I left the Count on the best of terms. He made me promise to keep him informed of anything interesting that I saw. That could have filled a book, I later discovered.

CHAPTER FOUR

THE RIDING ARTIST
Italy, 1895

I remember the first time I saw her. Some friends of mine had invited me to a small party. They had told me that a woman who specialised in choreographed riding exhibitions would be there, but frankly I hadn't given it much thought.

When she walked into the room, however, it was impossible not to notice her. It would be difficult to describe what she wore as a dress: it was more like a costume – an ensemble in different hues of red, embellished with a fine shawl edged with gold. The shawl

[50]

looked as if it was from India, and yet it did not.

She was a strking woman with thick, light-coloured hair that caught the colours of her shawl and blended with the colours of her skin. It didn't seem possible that anyone could contrive these dazzling visual effects of clothes and body. I also noticed that her scent somehow evoked the exotic origins of the fabrics she wore. Yet it was hard to believe that the complex way she appeared was just a coincidence.

She was at least fifteen years older than me, but I found her very attractive. Her body was elegant and athletic, and she moved with a kind of trained grace that I found to be an instant magnet.

During the course of the evening I contrived to speak to her, and, of course, our conversation fell into talk about riding. Somehow we got onto the subject of transitions. I felt a little proud of myself because we seemed to be agreeing that transitions were a very important measure of the quality of riding. Then she said something which I thought was odd. It also was intriguing. She told me that if I really wanted to learn about the highest quality of transitions, I should listen to music, and in particular I should especially study a very famous composer whom we both knew. I must have looked at her a little strangely because she continued to explain that this composer was a true master of transitions, of all kinds. She felt that if one could truly study transitions, one would see that a transition is a transition. The knowledge of them could be applied anywhere. I had to ask her to explain more.

'If a person studies one thing very well, and takes it very deep, that person can communicate with other deep students regardless of their respective expert subjects. The process is universal. That is why I contend that the process is more important than the subject. The paradox is that one needs a subject as a kind of password to get into the club. On the other hand, if a person studies many areas, many things, all superficially, that person ends up with a superficial knowledge. He can communicate well with all other superficials, but not with persons of deep knowledge. Superficial learning is too wide and flat for me,' she said. 'It is also limiting.

'In order to arrive at a deep knowledge, there will have to be at least some superficial study. So the deep student can, if he wishes, work in either world. The superficials can only work in one. One good deep student can often help another. That is a little of what I was talking about when we were discussing the genius of the composer's transitions, and the lessons embedded in them.'

She told me she was going to be touring again this year. She presented equestrian exhibitions at various venues throughout Europe. She had several months of practice ahead of her, which she was just starting. In these practices she would design and rehearse the new exhibition. She would then take it on a tour for some nine months before returning to her home in northern Italy. I was fascinated and when she invited me to come, see and be a part of the whole process, I knew I had to go.

My time with her ended up being one of the most important and most difficult segments of my riding education.

* * * * *

I arrived in Italy early in summer. I travelled by train to the village where she rented a small yard. I passed olive groves and poppy fields, the hills growing larger as we came closer to the edges of the Alps. Then, nestled among the steep vineyards with its stone and wood houses, the village appeared. In actual linear miles we were not far from the border with Switzerland.

She had a small complex with some pasture and a compact yard. She had five stallions in work and kept them in a row of boxes, so they stood side by side as they looked out over the half-doors. Near the yard, a small manège with grey sand and river gravel was terraced into a hill side. There on that tiny steppe she trained her horses.

I rented a room with meals from a young woman with two small children. The house was fairly large, one of about a dozen built around the small crossroads that made up the village centre. Nearby was a large communal well and water trough fed by an ever-flowing, clear, cold spring. During the day people came by to collect drinking water. Some women washed clothes. Several times a day small herds of goats were brought to drink. This appeared to be the nerve-centre for the small sprawling farms and cluster of houses that formed the village. In the background the high hills pushed up toward the foothills of forest below of one of the most formidable mountain ranges in the world.

Just living up there in that country was revitalising. It was fascinating to watch the designs for her riding displays come into being and eventually take on more and more definite form. She was a very good trainer and always thought of her horses first. In the beginning she just seemed to be riding and thinking. She would train certain movements on certain horses, and each would be exercised every day, but she seemed to be searching for an idea or a theme. In those first few weeks you could often see her depart from the normal practice routines and try a different pattern or an exercise in an odd place. She might stop on a horse and sit quietly, staring blankly. I found out later she was often thinking of music during those moments.

It was during one of those early sessions that I

remember her saying to me, 'People believe that facts and knowledge will help the world, but it is really *feelings* that will help the world. It is also feelings that will help one ride.' She was trying to explain her work or the differences between it and that of other trainers. But I don't think she realised that that was the whole reason why I was there. I guess she just didn't trust that I would make any sense of those early practices, which did appear somewhat haphazard and vague. The truth was that I most loved to watch it when it *was* so vague and she was brewing her concoctions. She was a riding alchemist, mixing this feeling with that, heating or cooling different expressions. It was exciting to see the smoke puffs of her inspiration swirl like clouds until some would join together gaining mass or form. Then all of a sudden, they would become solid and something recognisable would emerge from her experimentation. It got so I could almost feel it coming.

Sometimes, she would be quiet for a long time. At other times she would start talking right in the middle of her riding as if she were not only trying to explain it to me, but also attempting to verbalise it for herself. It seemed as if the words had to come out right there and then, as if she were a psychic medium.

'You see,' she said to me one day after a beautiful piece of piaffe, 'for so many people all there is to a movement is the anatomy of it. They study the names of bones or muscles, the pattern of the movement, with more and more intellectual explanations, as if they are scientists. If you do this and this you will get the movement. That's all there is to it. For me, movements have feelings first. There are emotional movements and powerful movements. Movements have colours and moods. You have to ride them differently. If you don't ride that way, the performance will look one-dimensional – like an orchestra would sound if it were comprised of only one instrument. I need bass feelings and trill feelings, ranges in emotion.

'A movement like piaffe has its roots in the mating dance of horses. It is a stallion's dance to attract a mare. It has sensual tension. It is about power, excitement, sex. It is not, and never should be, violent, because it is about love.

'If you ride the piaffe or passage without power and with weak mistakes instead of exuberant mistakes, you don't know anything about these movements. Or worse, you don't care. It doesn't matter to me if you know where each foot goes or which muscle does what. You have taken the piaffe out of its natural context. It doesn't make sense any more. It has turned into a parody. What you are doing does not glorify horses. It glorifies yourself, the human, on the horse. I believe you have to touch the soul behind every movement.

'When we take our tour to other countries, you will see riders pulling movements apart and making horses do crazy things. It saddens me, even sickens me, and I want to retreat up here. I want to stay here but I can't. I think those people would ride their horses upside down if they could. They are thrilled with the novelty of what they have created. There is a huge problem, however, because this is all at the expense of the horse's own culture. They mock the language of the horse. The life of the horse, the history of the horse, the movement of the horse. They have no respect for the horse, only an insatiable ambition of their own.'

As the summer wore on, I spent more and more time riding with her. I truly enjoyed it. She would use her training sessions as lessons. She could develop any technical movement from her own view or perspective and then get me to try to express that emotion or feeling.

[55]

She hated the practice sessions to be dull and wanted to see real effort and emotion. She once told me, 'If you want to be a soldier, that's fine – join the army. But if you want to be an artist, you have to put feeling and expression in your work.'

Different movements had stories behind them. For her the half-pass had a defensive flavour. 'Imagine a horse trotting down a road,' she said, 'and a wolf leaps out from the side. The horse arches its whole body and bounds forward and sideways. It is more of a feint. If the wolf were to come up from behind, the horse would gallop off using its superior speed. That is an extension – abandonment, almost fearful abandon. But a half-pass must have effort. It should almost startle. It is a graceful dodge.'

In her mind she said she could see the shape of a woman Flamenco dancer: her arms high above her head, her body in one slender long curve from her feet through the smooth arc of her ribs to her stretched arms and fingers, finishing with a sweep into the air. That is how the half-pass could feel to her.

She loved the pirouette most of all. She taught me that the pirouette is like a matador with his cape before him. His body is extended, as the bull, with its thousand-pounds-plus of power, moves into the magic of the thin drape. Just as the matador leads the bull, so the rider must lead the horse, using the lightest of reins and a firm, extended back and open chest. The bull turns the smallest of circles around the feet of the matador as the latter stretches his body line.

'When the pirouette is right,' she said, 'when it climbs high with all the weight collected, then, if at that point you glance down with your inside eye, you will see the inside foot of the horse. It will look like the slipper of a matador. You and the horse, the matador and the bull, will all become one, like a cyclone of power. You must learn to regulate it, to control it. Ask the bull to come in toward you. Close up the distance between you and power, and turn it in a sphere until it becomes a revolution. Get inside the eye of this image, and think. Keep thinking. Ride through every step. Never panic. Go steady. Control it.' I noticed that she always smiled when we were practising the pirouette.

'The shoulder-in', she told me, 'is like herbal tea. It is a potion with medicinal qualities.' She went on, 'When you ride it, let it go slow. Let it steep. Let it brew. You should never rush the shoulder-in. Give it a chance to work its magic. You have to use it every day. Half the value of tea like this is in the careful meditation during its preparation. Take your time preparing the shoulder-in. Then drink it slowly and don't stop using it when you feel better. Use it daily to promote the health of your horse.' To that end she never used the shoulder-in in her exhibitions. It had a more important purpose for her.

As time passed, the tour date was coming closer. I was intrigued by what I might see in other countries – the breaking up of movements, the out-of-control riders, the wild innovations. We talked a lot about what she had observed over the years. She told me she had a unique view of the equestrian world. At this time, it was a world almost completely dominated by men, mostly from the military. In the past there had been the occasional powerful woman, like a Marie Theresa, who had greatly influenced the horse world, but such women were, by and large, the exception.

Her father had been a powerful military man. Even now, long after his death, whenever she travelled to different cities, she usually visited one of his old compatriots, or one of them would feel he had to check on her. 'My military connections have allowed me to see many of the well-known riders and trainers at work,' she told me.

'Moreover, I have been able to observe some of them over a long period of time since I began watching them when I was a young girl.

'People have a habit of seeing a rider once, then filing away their impression in some comfortable place and labelling him that way forever. If you ask them about that rider years later they say, "Oh, yes, he does this or that," dismissing him with a one-sentence description. Certainly some riders do not grow or change, but the good ones do. A lot. It is amazing to see them or talk to them every few years. Their journey can be fascinating.

'There do seem to be two types of riders, though. One is the ambitious type, which seems more prevalent among younger officers, but is by no means restricted to them – there are plenty of older men who also seem obsessed with ambition and victory. When this first type are fighting in wars, they are not a problem. But in peace time, they can't seem to control themselves. They will invent violences. For them, competitions are like that. If things, even on a daily basis, get too smooth, they create pressures. They love to tell you what to do even if they have no control over you. They will show you what it is all about, what *they* can do, not what *you* might be able to do. They *need* you to see them. They need measurement and approval. They are in trouble when they are outside all the didactic support of the rules of the military.

'The other type,' she said, 'was like my father. They have been part of too much violence. They seem to be seeking something for themselves. They might tell you about it but they are not obsessed with showing everyone. This second type seem to be seeking the same thing: beauty. The more violence that has touched them, the more aggressively they seek the antidote in harmony and beauty. Even in this pursuit some of them retain their competitiveness. But all of them work hard. The peace they seek is no sleepy rest. Finding harmony is hard work.

'My father,' she said, 'often said it was a lot harder than war, just as to love is much harder than to hate.'

She felt this grouping into types explained a lot of the developments in riding. I was anxious for the chance to see this for myself, and I felt thrilled that she would be my guide.

As we came closer to the start of her tour, my duties became more involved. Two more horses were brought in so that there would be spares. I was in charge of all the horses' care, the grooms' travel arrangements, the supplies and equipment, etc. More logistical matters were sent my way even though I had no experience in this kind of lengthy travel. I was learning every day. Some days we would catch up with the workload and I would spend a summer evening sitting near the village spring just watching the sun go down. It was as peaceful as any time in my life.

During the practice sessions, the exhibition began to reveal itself. She started to bring in musicians to develop the score behind the whole performance. There were two – a cellist and a horn player. Some days she worked with just one and sometimes they both came. It was fascinating to watch them work together. The sounds of the music, first in short phrases and then in more and more complete pieces, would float into the afternoon or evening air. Sometimes during these practices I would hike over to the opposite hill, from which viewpoint I could barely see her riding but I could hear the horn drift. To me it was exciting to be part of the unfolding, the battling for direction, the nurturing and embellishing of an idea, or a feeling they were working to create. I was beginning to learn to love the work; the opening, the fixing, the hammering and the sawing of the work. She made me work hard, but I loved it. She taught me what she was after and listened to me. She let me be a real part of it. I was thrilled when I saw my humblest suggestions appear as little pieces in the work. She was like so many of the 'good ones'. She just wanted you to be honest – say something honest with all your might.

She had definite ideas as to how the horse and riding should integrate with the music. She would never have the music match any horse's rhythm of gait or footfalls. She felt the riding had to be able to counterpoint the music. There had to even be room for dissonance as well as harmony. 'If you follow the beat of the music,' she said, 'there can be no sophistication or complexity. It ends up looking and sounding like one hundred trombones on the Champs Elysées all playing the same tune. It is a marching band, not an orchestra. You can add more trombones if you wish, but the sound will not get more complex. It will only get louder. The effect is too banal. Furthermore, if you stay too close to the music, the horse ends up as another instrument. Nothing more than an implement of percussion. The music gets bigger than the horse.'

I felt she was exactly right. She would often show the musicians and myself what she meant. If the rhythm of the music and the rhythm of the horse stayed together, one couldn't stand it if the horse got out of sync. She said the audience would always feel that the horse had made a mistake. She was right, of course. It always appeared as if the horse was messing up the music.

She showed me how the counterpoint of the riding need not actually be a counterpoint to the rhythm of the music. It would just be differences in moods – the gentlest music for a powerful pirouette, for example. 'There are no rules,' she said. 'You experiment to see what works for you and for the audience. Never be afraid to challenge people with your art. Even dissonance at times will highlight and amplify harmony without adding more raw volume.

'We have to remember,' she would say quietly so that the musicians could not hear, 'that the music is secondary to our horses. We have to use musicians and their music in order to glorify the horse.'

As the days of the season grew a little shorter, the design began to gel. We were rehearsing the entire show. An odd feeling engulfed me. Everything seemed anticlimactic. We hadn't even started, and I had the strangely sad feeling that it was over. However, I could not afford to feel too much of anything for too long, because the reality of the logistics of travel and the first show had taken over my life. There were venues to formalise, bookings and livery to reserve, train passes to purchase, and so on and so on. We were going to start in Milan, then go to Geneva before the weather got too bad. On to Lyons, then a big stay in Paris. Brussels was next, then Amsterdam. We would go through Germany to Poland and continue east to Kiev. There we would turn south to Budapest, after which we would be starting home, travelling through Vienna and Salzburg. Our last show would be Venice.

And so it began, but much of it was a blur of very long days and nights – and so much to worry about. She was so good at travelling, but I felt I had an overwhelming responsibility to the horses. There was no question that this kind of life was hard on them.

During the tour very little changed. Obviously there was no place for the elixir of innovation. There was a choreography to stick to. Since we couldn't afford to take all the musicians with us, there were often new musicians to teach and fit in in different cities. I know the people loved her work but it was difficult to say how many had any *real* idea of what she was doing. Sometimes I wondered how she kept up her spirits.

Since many people already knew and admired her there were dinner requests and parties after performances. She was always the diva. She never faltered. I know she often had doubts and was discouraged by being asked the same tired questions; and she was dismayed by the often blatant presumptuousness she encountered. Nevertheless she could stay graceful and diplomatic throughout the repetitive onslaughts of ignorance.

I remember an incident one evening in Budapest as we were making our way back home. She opened up to me about herself and her motivations. We were in a café after one of the performances. It was a fairly typical scene but this particular evening seemed less pressurised. It was one of the last shows. I think we all sensed we were nearing the end. We were almost within sight of home.

We stayed late that evening. Everyone in the café was having a good time. In one part of the large room there was a group of workmen who had been drinking pretty heavily. At first, quietly, they began to sing a melancholy folk song. It was one of those typically ethnic national songs that when helped with a little alcohol unleashes the emotions of the most stoic of men. The song spread throughout the café until all the nationals participated. We did not know the words so we were respectfully quiet, although some of us did hum along.

I was sitting next to her and she turned to me and asked, 'Why do you think a song like that works that way?' I had not given it much thought. 'They are usually simple songs,' she continued out loud. 'If you sing them in another country, they won't get any kind of response. Even if you translate them so they would be relevant to another country, you still would not get this kind of reaction.

'Many people assume that there must be something

special in the song. But I have studied this, and it is not the song. Otherwise, the response to the song would be more universal. If you transpose these songs outside their borders, the lyrics can often be almost childlike.' She translated a few lines from some famous songs and out of their context they were powerless; whereas in their particular context, they would often be some of the most powerful music within a society.

'So how does this come about?' she asked me. I told her I wasn't sure. Slowly, with resignation in her voice, she said, 'They were all taught to love that song. From the time they were children,' she went on, 'it was carefully and specifically taught for many reasons, whether to represent love, or feelings of home and family, or of pride, nationalism, patriotism, whatever. That song is a vehicle to transport these often rich and deep feelings. The song can be a trip-wire to an explosion of associations. All those who have been taught this song share a common bond. Only those who have been taught it can participate in the brotherhood and sisterhood of these wealthy emotions. Tonight you and I don't know the song so we can only sit here and enjoy the sight and sounds of this gathering. But we can't be one with them. Any aesthetic ideas take hold or have effect only when the ground has been prepared ahead of time. A song can trigger your love for your homeland, your family, so many things. The song, like any art, can break down inhibitions, huge walls – the emotional fences of strong men and women. The song triggers a camaraderie which escalates beyond the original response. First a man responds to the song, then other men respond to the first, and then they all respond to the song. The magic is what gets involved in the song.' She looked at me with tears in her eyes.

'There is no hope for us if we don't teach all the songs

[63]

of the horses. It is not enough just to promote our particular art form. We must teach an appreciation of the horse and all the mythological connections which in the end is all of nature. If we don't succeed,' she said sadly, 'they'll just eat them. We have some obligation to our friends, the horses, if we think they and nature are important. We have to educate people's aesthetic awareness. This is why sometimes I have to move so far away from the technical plan. I don't hate technique, I love it. But it can cloud the issue and make some people look at the wrong thing. Technique will not make these men cry. There isn't a real singer in this whole place. The folk song is not an elaborate composition of technical prowess in music. It is an educated, common feeling. An appreciation.

'There isn't a magic piece of art that affects all people all over the world the same way,' she went on. 'People have to be trained to be hit by art. You train them in the medium you wish them to appreciate, and you train them with the medium you wish them to appreciate. So,' she concluded, 'I am always looking for new ways to catch their attention, enthral them, show them something that they can feel. To show them *why* they should care about horses.'

After that I knew exactly what she was trying to do, and I have never faltered from my belief that she was absolutely right.

CHAPTER FIVE

JANGALA
Maryland, 1960

I had learned to dislike the equestrian press, despite the fact that I myself was both a writer and a contributor. I felt they constantly avoided tough questions and ignored troublesome facts about equestrian personalities who basked in golden reputations. There had been several instances where riders had been arrested and convicted of crimes, and yet the equestrian press had either failed to report these stories or made excuses for those involved. It was the safest kind of journalism. I suppose I was as much at fault because I hated those personality pieces and would have nothing to do with them. Yet I did nothing to rectify the situation.

I was at my defensive best when a magazine sent a young reporter to interview me. I was expecting the usual, banal questions but she threw me off guard when she asked: 'Will you tell me about Jangala?'

'Who told you about Jangala?' I asked.

'Several people. They asked me not to mention their names. They said it was an interesting story.'

'Jangala is dead.'

'I know that,' she said. 'This is important to me. I'll put the notepad down. I won't even write about it if you will just tell me.'

'I don't like to talk about it – not for the reasons you might think. It is not painful or anything, but Jangala is really about the absence of words. I rode Jangala every day for almost twenty years. He was like a seeing-eye dog for a blind person. He took me to places I could never have gone by myself. I feel that talking about it demeans what happened.'

'Please, just a little bit about him. What did his name mean?'

'Jangala is Sanskrit for "impenetrable".'

'How did you get him? Will you at least tell me that much?' she implored.

'It's a long story,' I said.

'I have plenty of time. Please?'

My mind went back to the morning I first met Jangala. I could remember it with no distortion, even though I hadn't thought about it for a long time. Sometimes something would trigger the memory, and I could relive it – the smell, the cold air, the sounds. My recollection of it all was so complete. So I started to tell her about Jangala.

'My wife and I ran a small riding business. I taught riders and trained horses; she managed the yard and agented horses for sale. Our house and stables were close to each other, and near to a small road that wound through horse country and eventually came out onto an important north/south highway. That day, a lorry from a professional shipper from the south was due to arrive in the middle of the night to pick up a horse that my wife had sold. It was nothing unusual. The driver said he would phone when he was fifteen minutes away. He planned to stop, load up the horse, and be off again to return south.

'Around three o'clock in the morning, the phone rang. My wife answered it. I weakly asked if she needed my help, and was ecstatic when she said no. I turned over and went back to sleep. Shortly thereafter I faintly heard the sound of a heavy diesel engine coming down the road, and then idling in front of the stable. I was barely awake, but I could hear the motor running. The transaction seemed to be taking a long time, but what was really annoying was this constant, rhythmic banging. Finally I thought the truck must have some mechanical problem, and the driver was pounding on something to fix it.

'I got up, dressed, and went outside. There was a heavy mist. We lived in a little valley beside a stream, and often in the summer and autumn nights, the fog would build up around us. It felt cold to me, probably because I was not fully awake. As I approached the barn, I could see my wife and the driver talking inside under the yellow lights. I could also see the lorry idling on the edge of the road, shaking with each bang from inside. The source of the noise was now clear – it was a kicking horse. Its banging had not ceased, even for a moment's respite, since the lorry had pulled up and parked there.

'When I went into the barn, they could see by the look on my face that I was perplexed. The driver apologised and told me that, if we didn't mind, he was to rendezvous with another lorry at our farm. He was to unload the rogue that was on his lorry and put it on onto another, bound for New York. The rogue horse was destined for Australia to run with a band of mares. As soon as the switch was made, he would load our horse and be off. He told us that the kicking horse on board was truly a rogue and he thought it might be tricky to switch him onto the other lorry. I became intrigued and asked to look at the horse. "He's boxed in," I was told. I must have looked at the driver oddly.

'When I walked into the large, well-lit box, I couldn't see the horse at first. Then I noticed that the thudding was coming from a small, wooden stall at the back corner of the horsebox. A specially constructed pen was completely sealed to the ceiling on three sides. At the front there was about a foot of space near the ceiling, and inside this wooden-sounding drum was a horse.

'I could see steamy breath coming out the narrow space at the top. I was completely fascinated, and was about to climb on a couple of bales of hay to look inside when I heard the second lorry coming down the road. All the while the pounding was incessant.

'Without seeing the horse I went back out. Our driver talked to the other. Neither was keen on the manoeuvre ahead but they decided on a plan. They were to open the side doors of each truck, and park them as close as possible to one another so there would only be a very small space between them. At that point one of them would dismantle the stall, keeping behind the plywood barrier, and drive the horse from one lorry to the other. Once the horse was on the second lorry, they would move quickly, shut the doors and leave the horse loose inside until they reached New York. I was intrigued as to what they were going to do when they got to New York, but I thought, one step at a time.

'When both men kept hesitating as to who would turn

the horse loose, I volunteered. A certain excitement rushed through me. It was a very odd, very familiar, very good feeling. It invoked one of my earliest memories – the attraction and the excitement of wild animals.

'My family maintain that I am magnetically drawn to animals, and always have been, even before I had any intellect to know why. My mother told me how an angry goose once dragged me around my grandmother's yard when I was two, but it did not phase me. I grew to love birds as one of my favourite animals. At four, my recollections are of animals, not people. And ever since I was a child, I remember that same inexplicable feeling, almost like laughter coming up from way down deep inside me, when encountering a special animal.

'I went in. I planned an escape route and then climbed on a hay bale to look over the partition at the horse. When I saw him, I was at that place from which I want to die. Charged, but quiet. I was where I belonged. It was something I knew I could do. The horse was in a seething rage. His head was held down tightly by two heavy chain cross-ties. He wore a heavy iron muzzle. His eyes rolled back and up as he stared at me. He actually stopped kicking. His eyes transfixed.

'I reached in slowly over the top of the wood partition. It was hot in his stall. I didn't speak to him. I must have sensed that he was not about to respond to words. I gingerly reached to the side of his halter and held the huge snap in my right hand. Quietly I unhooked it.

'I remember thinking it was odd that he hadn't moved a muscle. He stayed frozen, as if he were still hooked up. I moved my arm slowly to the other side. When I carefully took the snap in my hand, he moved his eyes, and I knew I had met a very smart horse. When my hand had been on the first snap, the other chain had prevented his head from going toward me. He hadn't moved until my arm was committed. Now, with my hand on the snap, he simply moved toward the chain, which had slackened. As I attempted to finish my task, he very slowly and very deliberately pinned my forearm to the wall. There was no speed, no fury. He stared at me again. At first I felt the pressure of the steel muzzle increasing. I thought he was going to break my arm. I was wearing a heavy woollen shirt-jacket. Then I realised he was pushing all the space out of the muzzle until his teeth were at the edge. Then, as if he were grazing tenderly on bits of grass, he began to chomp at the fragments of my wool sleeve, pulling more and more material into the wire muzzle cage. He was going to eat my arm, and I couldn't move.

'There was nothing I could reach with my free hand to help me. Finally I worked my left arm up to the top of his stall bars, and as fast and hard as I could, I clapped his ear. That startled him, and for a brief moment he released his grip. I yanked my arm free, but not before I unsnapped the second snap. He was free. As quickly as I could I took off the front wall, and opened his stall. Pulling the partition back with me, and keeping it between him and me, like a huge riot shield, I didn't have to chase him. He saw the opened door and jumped out of his stall right into the second lorry. I followed him and positioned a wooden board to block his exit from the second lorry. The drivers quickly drove the lorries apart so I could close and lock the side doors. As soon as there was space, he knew it and came crashing into my barrier. He knocked me down and onto the road, the board falling on top of me. I could hear his clattering feet on the tarmac surface. He was free. I was stunned. Lying on the road I realised had just shaken hands with Jangala.'

'What happened next?' the journalist asked.

'The first in a series of riddles that lasted for almost

twenty years: he ran a short way down the road, turned, then ran back up the road and into my barn. It was a great old barn with thick stone walls. He ran into one of the back stalls, stood in a darkened corner, and someone shut the door behind him. There was no way anyone was going into that stall. There was a monster in that cave. The lorry drivers made some phone calls, and a little while later they asked me if I wanted the horse. The owner did not want him back. Everyone had had enough. He was clearly dangerous and unmanageable.'

'How did you reach him? I mean, I know you reached him somehow,' she asked.

'Look,' I said. 'It's all rather involved. As I told you, it doesn't fit with words.'

I couldn't hide my irritation with her. I didn't mind that she was curious, but I didn't feel she was really trying to understand the whole perceptual shift – maybe she couldn't. I had been in this situation before, trying to explain a new analogy, using different phrases which all turned out to be completely useless, but there was nothing else, no other perceptions, I could use. I had always known that the essential struggle, the purest struggle, for any teacher is between words and experience. The two will never be the same. Yet I seemed always to be trying to make myself understood – to let someone feel what I had felt and seen.

'Did you treat him with kindness? Is that how?' she went on.

'In the beginning I treated him fairly and with respect. It was not out of some altruistic idea of his worth as a living animal, or some philosophical or moral approach. I treated him with respect because he demanded it. He was dangerous. That stall he was in had three stone walls and one wooden plank one. On one of the first occasions I went into his stall with him, I somehow got behind him.

I knew it was a mistake. I tried to manoeuvre myself quietly and quickly toward the door, but it wasn't going to work. All of a sudden he started kicking with both hind feet. I immediately crowded his rump so I wouldn't be at the end of his reach where his hooves would hit with full force. I felt him hit one of my knees, but it wasn't too bad. The boards were cracking and splintering behind me. He kept kicking. By a stroke of pure luck I somehow got out the door, and with only a bruise on my knee. I couldn't take him for granted for a minute. You see, he was not interested in kindness. For him, the touch of a stick or a soft hand was equally repulsive. Have you ever been around a couple going through a divorce? Have you ever been in love with someone and fallen out of love?'

She looked a little embarrassed but she admitted that yes, she had. I wasn't sure how deeply she knew this.

'Then you must have seen how touch can change. Touch can be welcome, sought after, exciting. But something happens, and the touch of the same temperature, the same pressure, an identical physical phenomenon can feel heavy, painful, intrusive. I learned so much from Jangala about touch. People are so foolish. They practise touch to seduce, as if your technique will make you be loved. Haven't they ever noticed that some of the most passionate love, that of young lovers, comes from those most inexperienced at touch? Love, and to a lesser degree acceptance of more base pleasures, are based totally on reception. Technique and intention are meaningless without willing reception.'

She interrupted me. 'You know,' she said, 'once when I was very young, I had a dog. I remember that dog as always being with me. One day I reached down to stroke him, and he bit my hand. The bite burned, and my finger was bleeding. I cried and cried. My father thought my reaction was completely out of proportion. It wasn't that much of a bite, but I was too young to explain, and maybe I didn't understand or realise why. But what hurt so much was that I felt my friend had betrayed me. It must have been my first recollected experience with what you are talking about. My touch unreceived. Maybe it is base to compare that emotion to the complexities of someone's divorce, and even falling out of love. But I haven't had a clearer feeling of that pleasure/pain all rolled into one quick event.'

'I hope you never know any worse pain, or ever feel any stronger rejection,' I said to her, 'but the odds are great that you will. There is no difference, though. The scale may escalate, the stakes get higher, but the lesson is the same. Think about the ramifications in all ways. Not just if you are or aren't received, but how much you will or won't receive. Because you can respond in many the different ways, you can be like Jangala. He tried to make me afraid to touch him. He taught me so much about reception. Do you give up? Do you turn away? There are infinite ways. Do you make yourself unapproachable, isolate yourself from being touched? On the other hand, you can project and project yourself until your attempts are suffocating. If you touch the same spot over and over again, it becomes irritating, even tortuous. This is a complicated matter, but you have to learn as much as you can about reception. Listen, watch all the time. Become aware. Develop empathy. All the great horsemen and women had keen powers of empathy. If you are in dangerous places, it can save your life. It is also a powerful aphrodisiac.

'Horses are very quiet animals. You will need to learn about and develop empathy. After a long time you can tell by their scars where they have been, and what has happened to them. Like old walruses gouged with scars of battles, horses have these notches inside and out. Little by little, without a single word, you will find out what their experiences have been. You won't need a location. Don't become some silly detective looking for the facts of their lives, what country they are from, who their owners were. This is all meaningless. Everyone is from somewhere else, for God's sake, but what kind of place was this animal from? If he tried to kick your brains out the first time you met him, you can usually assume it was not a good place. But don't trap yourself with even those seemingly obvious observations. Learn to go deeper, and the best way to go deep is to limit your presumptions. Feel your way through. Touch your way through. You see, these are just some of the things about touch that Jangala showed me. This is how he started talking to me.'

'What do you mean he started talking to you?' She looked at me sceptically, but also a little warily, as if the interview were getting a little strange or uncomfortable for her.

'First, let me say that through this touch he escorted me into what was, for me, a new heightening of my senses. Very powerful, very complete.'

'I am not sure I follow you,' she said.

'We need to learn new ways to use our senses. All of our senses. All of the time. That is what I began to learn. I began to increase my powers of perception. This is not as bizarre as it might seem. We all have a passport to this seemingly mysterious level of sensual awareness and existence. You do not have to learn anything new. You have to awaken a gift that you already have! You see, your passport to this learning is the fact that you are also a living animal. You are not a machine. We are incredibly equipped to go on this journey with the horse. But to embark on this journey, you have to do one important thing first, and that is to reduce the dominance of your language, the linguistic monopoly of your senses.'

She looked astonished. 'You don't mean that literally you talked with Jangala – I mean, like you asked him a question and he answered?'

'I don't mean to disturb you, but that is exactly what happened. You are making a big mistake if you think that communication happens only with words. The Zen follower might make the case that it is *because* of words that direct communication often does not exist. The incredible thing is that once I took this step, I began to realise that practically the entire world, except man, communicates and maintains complex relationships of all types without words and sometimes with very little sound. We are making ourselves un-understandable to the rest of the world by insisting and becoming totally dependent on our words. You see, one of the reasons I got tired of talking about Jangala and telling the story of how I met him, is because people love the story. It is like a fable, and what people want from a fable is something mystical. They'd have liked me to have said something divine to him, or to have spoken like Allah, breathing into the nostrils of the first Arabian horse. That would have made it simple, really. They could go home with the tale of Jangala, the horse and the man. What actually happened was even more magical to me, but required years and years of psychological and physical toil on both our parts. How it ends up is the horse is a man, and the man is a horse. Up to this point the Jangala story is fabulous but it is nothing more than the taming of a wild animal. Do you know what the expression *dompteur versus dresseur* means? In classical riding it is the tamer versus trainer. I was the tamer in the beginning, but this horse, more than any other, taught me to be the trainer of a dressage horse.

'I have tamed many animals. I was a falconer. I tamed

irascible goshawks and flighty falcons. I tamed monkeys, a fox and a wolf. Once I tamed a feral dog, and I have even tamed fish. In the end, it was always a man, and a wolf, a man and a hawk, a man and an ape. Only in dressage did the animal and the man merge. We became something more and different from either one of us alone. When you meet a *dresseur* they know that the centaur is no myth.'

'Is it possible to tell me how this starts?' she asked. 'I am stuck on this talking thing. How did he talk to you? I am fascinated as to how this developed?'

'When I eventually led Jangala, then lunged Jangala, then rode Jangala, one of the first awarenesses that came back to me was gravity. This is perhaps *the* most amazing force in our lives, but we often forget about it or take it for granted. For a human the first seduction of a powerful horse is the apparent freedom from gravity he gives us. At least we are released from its powerful limits on our mobility. But all this is very egotistical, very egocentric.

'However, you quickly realise that how you sit on the horse affects how the horse can move. Soon you are forced to appreciate what a burden you are to the horse. You come to an impasse, and you are set up to see that the first step in communication is to listen. If you are in a strange land and its people speak a strange language, you will have to listen first. If you speak first, *they* will have to listen. If they have no interest in you or your language, the process stops. Certainly Jangala had no interest in me. I had to listen, but obviously not for sounds.

'He immediately forced me out of perceptual habits. He was not the first horse I had trained, so I was not totally ignorant of his language. If I had been, he would have been unreceptive to all my points of feeling. My reception had to be heightened, to be trained. He trained me, and in a perverse way he trapped himself. I guess the one thing I can say for myself is that he underestimated my persistence.

'You ask, did he answer questions? If you formulate a question, you are using words. I did things, and he responded. For example, in the simplest sense if I pulled on a rein, maybe he would pull back, maybe he would stiffen a back muscle or a hind leg. He responded to actions of my body with his body. Sometimes he initiated actions with his body, which elicited a reaction from mine. I had to learn what he was doing. I had to learn to feel every part of him in order to make sense of what he was communicating. What was going on might resemble a tennis match at the speed of light. If you filmed a tennis match and tracked the paths of the two players in a graph, placing a dot for the location of each shot and then connecting these dots, the match would look like a weaving. And the thread would weave a story. This graph or garment might be a tangible representation of the tennis match.

'Likewise, we could have made a graph of Jangala's and my interactions, but both would be nothing more than tracks in the sand. They would be past references to something that had already taken place. What actually happens might look like a dance. But in the beginning the interaction is often random, spontaneous, and mostly discordant. When you think about it, this is a description of fighting: two bodies engaged in spontaneous and discordant interaction. The art of riding is to choreograph this movement and to gain control of it by repetition. The art is to make the fight into a dance, and in this case the dance is that of the mythical centaur. The dance is not of one participant or the other. It is something new, and it is a representation of an invisible harmonious action and reaction. The choreography is the visible part, and yet it is meaningless because the real story is the interaction. The centaur represents all the feeling, all of the senses. If you idealise patterned movements, figures and geometric shapes, you will never be a *dresseur*. In other words, instead of being a painter, you would become a collector of paintings. If you talk without listening, you cannot communicate. Jangala made me understand movement, not just the movements of dressage. He taught me the movement in dressage.'

'Can you give me an example?' she asked.

'All right. Let's take a familiar problem and see what he taught me. Have you ever felt how some horses can pull on the left rein and it feels like they have a way to directly pressure the bursa in the point of your shoulder? If you have, you know exactly what I mean. It is a searing pain like a spasm. Sometimes, the horse doesn't have to pull on the rein very hard. It seems to be more the way he pulls – a steady, dull draw. Your arm fatigues, and soon there is this pointed pain. Once it starts, you have to rest the arm, but it seems that the moment you pick up the rein, it comes howling back. I knew I had to loosen Jangala on that rein, and I was persistent. So I held the rein. I found that after the arm spasms and goes numb, one loses a lot of dexterity but the pain subsides. So I held onto Jangala thinking that whoever was more stubborn would win.

'It was too easy for him. He kept his weight shifted a little to the front on that shoulder, and he let me try to hold up the world. He didn't snatch at the rein, but he didn't let go either. I got stronger and probably so did he, but after endless daily battles, all of which I lost, I began to understand what he was doing, and how he was getting to me.

'I started to use my left leg to make him bend around it. If you curve a horse's body the distance from the mouth to the tail decreases. When I could get him to bend from my leg, he momentarily would let go of that rein and therefore also my arm. I began to use my leg with as much determination as my arm. I found that a bigger muscle just takes a little longer to seize, and when it does it hurts more than a little muscle.

'At first, Jangala resisted my leg pressure and leaned into it. I found if I used the leg in conjunction with a turn I could get him off balance and it was easier to move him away from the leg pressure. My success, however, was short-lived. The chess match continued. Once he learned to go sideways away from my leg, he simply slid over and avoided my left leg touch. He then ran away from it fish-tailing sideways. I had to use my other leg to check the overzealous response. Furthermore any relief from my left rein pressure was temporary, because now I had to help my right leg and stop the sideways slide with my right rein. He was back in the hands.

'I decided to block his sideways slide by moving him off my left leg, but along a wall. It worked and I started to get some relief on the heavy left rein, but only as long as we were moving. I had one big problem. I couldn't stop him. So I learned to curve and recurve his body with my legs to induce a curve and control it with the checks and balances of my other leg and the wall. I learned you can't pull a curve in or out with your hands, because the neck will bend easily by itself.

'I could relieve the stiffness of his left side by riding in a curve along a straight line. If I wanted him to move off my leg, he obliged but he kept his balance out on the shoulders. I couldn't tell this until I tried to stop him and then I felt all the weight in front. Of course, I had perceived a sideways or lateral shift of weight and now I was face to face with the world of longitudinal shifts of weight. I started using intermittent tugs of the reins and complete stops to give my arms some relief and to ask him to stop more lightly. If I kept his hind legs active, trying especially to push the left hind under, and took tugs on the reins, paying attention not to let him bend his neck too much, he was forced to step into a channel I had created. If I was careful to curve him with my left leg and not pull his head into the turn or curve, then I wouldn't pull him onto his shoulders, and he would scoot his left hind leg up under his body. Then I would get relief in my arm. If he got heavy in the right rein, I simply went the other way.

'Later on, of course, I realised that Jangala had taken me step by step through the historical development of the shoulder-in. The Duke of Newcastle in the 1600s tried to free his horses in the shoulders by side-stepping them in a circle. De la Guerinière came along later and found that if he took the side-step along a straight wall it had the enigmatic effect of collecting the horse and collecting or re-balancing him a little to the rear. That way he could get the shoulders and front end freer than the Duke of Newcastle ever thought possible. Even if you read Guerinière's advice, you will still have to go through the process yourself to learn how to do it.

'Jangala took me through the movement isolating an aid by fatiguing it and thereby making me use something else. Now you can say that is just normal training, and all of this is not unusual, that it is just the exercise working. But Jangala could have stopped me, really **stopped** me at any point in this lesson. He could have reared, which he did later, but not then as it was not in the plan. He blocked me and frustrated me until I mastered another and another muscle nuance. The shoulder-in was a little symphony of muscle movements. He taught me every kind of movement that way. One step after another. My repertoire of muscle, ligament and mental memory accumulated. It was some deal. I saved his life and he taught me everything.'

She questioned me further: 'Did it become easier as you went along? Did he become your friend?'

'Of course, he was my friend, but I never thought of him as a brother. He was a father figure or maybe a great uncle. And no, it never became any easier. He was a great teacher. He was strict and demanding, an absolute stickler for detail every day, every movement. The aid had to be right.'

'And if it wasn't?' she asked.

'He would grab you and go through the hole you had missed and attack your opening. He'd stiffen. Basically he would pinpoint your awareness on your mistake in some dramatic way. As he trained me, he got even more particular. The degrees of strength or speed of reaction became very important. Not enough effort on my part, he'd ignore me. Too much, and he would rebuke me sharply for being crude. I remember, for example, that toward the end of our training he could do a beautiful piaffe pirouette, but it had to be just right. If you tried to rush him and push it around a little too fast, and I mean a little, he would hit the rein as if it were an electric fence, and stand straight up. He never turned over, but you got the message. Lighter, ride lighter. Be more aware!'

'And this lasted for twenty years?!' She seemed amazed.

'Yes.'

'And why in the world did you persist? Are you slightly masochistic?' She looked puzzled.

'No. Don't be silly. The answer to that is easy. You see, of course, I would get sick of his perfectionism, but take that piaffe pirouette for example. When it unfolded correctly, when I did it well enough that he approved, when I earned his respect, we moved in harmony and strange other things would happen.

'I felt concentration like a drug. The rhythm of the movement could become almost hallucinogenic, just as

[81]

drumming can heighten your senses. I could hear birds very clearly in the middle of the work. For years a mocking bird lived in the trees beside the riding arena, and if he would start his litany of songs, I could hear each song with no other distractions as if it were the only sound.

'Once I heard a different sound very high in the sky, and I saw a perfect skein of snow geese. They are fairly rare for us and the sound is different from the Canada geese, which are plentiful. I heard their muted jazz trumpet improvisations coming straight out of the sky, miles away. Remember, sound is slower than light; nonetheless, a little later, I saw them as they made a slight turn. The sun struck them against the cloudless blue sky. They exploded like diamonds, sound turning to light.

'Other times, I could actually *feel* the consistency of the sand under his feet. I could feel the depth of it, or if the sand was moist and held me well, or if it were too dry and broke away. I knew exactly how deep I was sinking with each step, and I could bounce myself off it on days when its weight was perfect and its texture firm. I knew its temperature and could taste its salty grit. I could feel the ocean where it had come from.

'If we travelled across the grass, there were times when his feet would crush the blades and an almost acidic scent would trail up behind us. On certain days in the spring in the morning when the air was wet and heavy, I could feel movement on my skin. I could feel the power of our motion inside the atmosphere, and some days this atmosphere could be dripping with the perfume of honeysuckle and locust tree blossoms - their distinct sweet jasmine aroma. In this alchemist's reduction, I remember when I fell in love for the first time. Sometimes, later, the scent would change to wild roses and privet blossoms. These sophisticated smells would creep around the piaffe and I could feel all dimensions of space – the air behind me, at the sides and in front of my face. Some days it would change. I swear I often had the strongest sensation of the smell of freshly baked bread floating across the outdoor school. I would have this satisfying feeling of eating warm, moist bread right in the middle of a ride.

'Sometimes I had such acute vision. I could identify insects flying across the arena as if they were in slow motion. I once followed a flying grasshopper for four consecutive fifteen-metre circles. It would land in front of us and then fly up with its dry striped wings, and then land right on the circle track and fly again, around and around until I guess it got bored.

'There were the many, many times when I felt weak or ill and I knew if I could get myself on my horse, I would be OK, and I was. He cured me every time people made me weary. He constantly freed me from the suffocating demands of society. He wouldn't let me become another cultural soldier.

'That is why I did it. To feel deeply, you have to **feel** deeply. When I was a little boy, I went to church every Sunday, confession every Saturday. I knew the biographies of the saints. I memorised long pages of prayer in Latin and in English. My little body vibrated under the tones of the powerful church organs. I served priests and I served nuns. I lit candles and burned incense at weddings, baptisms, funerals – and you want to know something? I never had a religious experience until I rode Jangala, who looked like something contrived by the devil. Jangala was my priest and horses became my religion.'

CHAPTER SIX

JOBAJUTSU
near Kyoto, 1970

In retrospect I realise my time in Japan was not about fighting, although every aspect of that adventure concerned fighting. I went in order to learn about an archaic form of fighting. During that time I felt increasingly destined for an imminent battle, which seemed to bring me back again and again to a state of agitation or, rather, confusion. Yet it was not what it seemed at all. It was one of the most difficult expeditions I could remember.

It started when a friend of mine who was teaching at a school in Japan sent me a letter. He told me one of his

fellow faculty members had a son who was one of only
two students learning riding from an old Japanese master.
He knew how much these things interested me and was
sure that I knew a lot more than he did about what this
man was teaching. In any case, the old riding instructor
seemed to be a genuine master and that in itself was rare
because my friend knew of no other riding teachers.
Furthermore, horses to ride were quite rare in this part of
the world.

He was, of course, absolutely right that these things
interested me. I had heard of *Jobajutsu,* the martial art of
horsemanship, but it was nothing more than a historical
footnote. The idea that it might still be alive somewhere
was too much for my curiosity.

Several things had conspired to force me into action, I
later discovered, but right then I just had to try to see
something that might soon be gone from this earth
forever. I asked my friend to explore the possibilities of
my having a chance to experience this work. When I
received word that I was welcome, I began to make
arrangements to go.

After considerable arranging and arduous travel, I
found myself approaching the old man's farm. My friend
drove me out to meet him. It was a forty-five minute ride
from the small city where my friend lived and taught. As
we drew closer, the country began to open up to some
carefully cultivated hill farms. The old man's little farm
complex was situated beside a ravine that dropped steeply
in places to a strong-flowing narrow creek. There was a
small house and some outbuildings, including a little
stable that housed his horse, and a small tea-house that
was set close to the brook.

Scattered around were what looked like an odd assort-
ment of bonsai trees gone wild. Once carefully pruned
and shaped, the trees retained their trained shapes at the

bottom, but all the new growth had branched out unattended. It reminded me of forests in which deer populations eat all the tender cedar branches as high as they can reach. Over the years the trees acquire a carefully manicured look up to a uniform distance from the ground, above which the full growth is resumed.

Our first meeting was cordial but rather formal. His two students, polite teenagers, were both there. Everyone respectfully referred to him as Sensei, teacher. He was quite humble and insisted that he had little to offer me, but I was welcome and he would oblige me in any way that he could.

In my time I had seen many schools covering a large range, but this had to be the smallest school of all: one teacher, one horse, two students. Definitely, it was the most basic. He invited me to come out riding the next morning. For my part I tried to be polite, but was careful not to show any feelings one way or the other.

I returned the next day and found him alone. He saddled up his horse, then he looked at me, looked at the horse, looked at me again, and then looked at himself. Then, in wonderful acting as if he were reading my mind, he said, 'Pitiful little school.' With a slight smile on his face he added, 'Just think how pitiful you must be as a student to come half way around the world to this pathetic little place.' We both laughed.

He and I walked the horse up to a long grassy field. After we talked and the horse was warmed up from the walk, he asked me to ride. It was a small horse, with no particularly outstanding characteristics. Certainly, by this stage in my riding experience, it was not the calibre of horse I had grown accustomed to. Although it had a short trot with a little stiffness in the back, I had no trouble sitting to it. The canter was better and the horse was very straight and could go almost perfectly straight with very little guidance. My suspicion was that this had something to do with being able to shoot a bow off its back while galloping, which was a part of Jobajutsu.

I did not want to be presumptuous, so after a brief ride through the field I rode the horse back to the old man to thank him for the honour of letting me ride his horse. I told him his straightness was impressive. I was not prepared for the man's reaction. He began to rave about how well I could sit. I am sure he had never seen a rider from the West, and certainly not someone schooled in dressage. I don't think he realised the countless hours we spend on the lunge line and riding without stirrups. He was so effusive with his praise and compliments that I began to get internally suspicious. Was he setting me up for something? Was he putting me on? He wanted to know who trained me and how we practised. I tried to explain everything. Then he caught me by surprise. He asked me if I would help him to get his students to learn to sit like I did. If I would do that, in return, he would help me in any way that he could.

There was something about him that I quickly grew to like. He seemed both wise and humble. He had a sense of humour, which gave you the feeling that he had a genuine interest in you. He told me if I wanted to learn to shoot the bow I would probably have little trouble since sitting quietly and strong was half the battle. Somehow I doubted this.

We went back to his little tea-house. He built a fire in a small pit in the middle of the room and prepared the tea in a careful ritual. He told me about the sitting position for meditation and the martial arts. Apart from my legs tiring from being bent, I was comfortable in the position. It was similar to sitting on a horse, especially through my back.

He asked me if I had any questions. I had some very

nagging ones, which were part of the reason I had come to learn about warfare and fighting from him. But I couldn't seem to formulate them. So I kept my questions more to the point of my immediate study. I told him that I had read and heard how, especially in archery, the students were instructed to try to *not* hit the target. I asked first how one could get better at something if one didn't try, and secondly why avoid the target?

He smiled slightly at me. 'Whatever gave you the idea that we wouldn't try? All these teachers want their students to try with all their strength to get the form right, not necessarily whether they hit the target. When these teachers talk about not hitting the target, they do not say "try not to hit the target". They say, "don't try to hit the target". There is a big difference. The point is you don't try to hit the target, but neither would you try not to hit the target. The emphasis is to take the student's attention away from outcome.

He went on, 'If you think of ten very successful people and you believe that outcome is an accurate reflection of what goes on before it, then one would say that all ten of those people must be hard workers, intelligent, good people. All would have the qualities which can lead to success. Obviously unless you know very different kinds of people than I do, this is not so. Some people inherit their success without a single day's work. Some steal their fortunes. Some find it, and a very few earn it. The issue of outcome can be a very thorny one which can actually delay or even paralyse the progress of proper practice.'

He told me he knew of one masterful teacher who was so tired of his students worrying about the outcome of their shots instead of their form and the process, that he made huge targets and brought them within a few feet of his archers. It was virtually impossible to miss the target, so his students would have to spend more time focusing on proper technique forms, and their breathing. 'Outcome,' he said, 'is certainly not a fair reflection of effort.'

I told him that in my society the pressures to win at something were very great. Part of the reason I came was to learn to defend myself against these pressures.

'This is not unique to your society,' he told me. 'Since man began chasing woman and woman chasing man, the pressures have been great. Outcomes became important and they were placed on every other aspect of living. But there is more to life than just desires. However, if you must have a winner, you must have a loser. People who think this way begin to divide all life into categories all the time. Life is not so neatly divisible. Nor does outcome necessarily tell you anything about how it came about. So we teach more about the process. And these teachers teach more about shooting the bow, living a life. Let outcomes take care of themselves.'

I felt I was just scratching at the surface, listening to him. I told myself to pay attention. Maybe I could learn how to practise.

After a while I developed a routine. When I arrived in the morning I gave each of the young men a half-hour lunge lesson. Sensei loved to watch these practices, although he rarely said a word. Then we might go to practise shooting the bows. This was not the easiest thing, because these bows had a strong tension and were physically demanding to shoot. Although I knew nothing of archery, I could see he was trying to prepare his students for shooting the bow while riding. I did not know what to do with the bow, but I had an advantage because I had spent years being lunged with hands free or in exercises using my hands in such a way that they would not disturb my seat, or vice versa.

* * * * *

His tea-house, like a lot of Japanese art, paid homage to the irregularities of Mother Nature by deliberately being constructed asymmetrically. It was purposefully set in the woods near the running stream, so that the sound of the water could soothe those inside with a feeling of being deep within a forest.

One day he asked the two students and me to join him for tea. He prepared the brew as always with regular care and ritual. In his odd collection of cups he poured each of us a near-full cup but asked us not to drink yet. He then asked that we sit comfortably but solidly in the sitting position for meditation. This position is almost mechanically identical to sitting on a horse, except that on the floor one's legs are folded up. He often used the term 'riding position' in place of the traditional meditation position, especially with me. He then said he was going to leave and come back, but no matter what happened we were not to let the tea spill on the floor. He looked sternly at his two students. He reminded them that this tea-house was built by his grandfather, and was given by his father to him. He got up and told us to wait until he got back.

There was an air of apprehension when he left. The young students tried to control themselves, but they were nervous. Because I was taller and because of where I was sitting, I could see out the corner of the window of the little house. Quietly Sensei had gone to the stable to fetch his horse. He was leading it toward the tea-house. I could see his face; he was practically giggling. Then he disappeared out of sight. I betrayed no emotion but was still very curious. All of a sudden the whole building shook. In this land of earthquakes, buildings are often built lightly so that if they do collapse, it is better to have a bamboo wall fall on you than one of stone or iron. I saw the students visibly startle. They had no idea what was causing the building to shake.

The teacher backed the horse slowly into the building, bumping the corner again and again. As the horse repeatedly collided with the tea-house, cups started falling. There was considerable movement inside. Each time the building shook, the fire would erupt with a small shower of fine sparks. We all sat as still as possible and during the whole time no one spoke a single word. Each of us tried to keep to the orders of the afternoon. I had no real trouble keeping the tea from spilling, but I attributed this to my addiction of coffee drinking which I did in every location and on every kind of travel mode. The two young men had a terrible time. Both tried hard to hold the cups tightly but both spilled a lot – probably from nerves as much as from the motion. One of them, trying to keep to the master's orders, held his cup over his clothes so that the spilt tea did not hit the floor but instead covered his pants. The other had no chance of even trying to balance the cup in front of him.

Finally the commotion stopped. The building was quiet again. I am sure they thought Sensei was mad. It was obvious that he was behind the disturbance, but they could not tell what he was doing. After a while the master came back and with a stern face examined each of us. He looked at the puddle on the tea-house floor in front of one of his young students. The young man stood silently humiliated. The second student's clothes were stained. The master looked at him less harshly. Then he looked at me. I remember it well because from that moment on he called me 'horseman'.

He said, 'Only the horseman has the hands to shoot the bow. The horseman has not spilled a drop because the horseman knows that to keep the tea still, the hand must move. If you try to keep the hand still, the tea becomes a volcano.' He let his face relax. He told them the spilled tea would add character to the house. Besides, he would now have a good story to tell his visitors at tea time. He had relieved most of the tension.

I realised it was a masterful lesson. I had learned this floating hand technique actually from riding, holding the reins. I had learned that in order to affect the bit, to keep it still, or to move it exactly, the hand must have fine control. It is never still or dead, but always is in some kind of searching/feeling action. Even in apparent stillness, there is always motion. Sometimes almost imperceptible motion. The master had seen that from my first ride, and he wanted to find a way for me to help his students. 'Only in death is there stillness,' he had told them.

He went on, 'If you try to shoot the arrow your way, it will be a dead effort – restrictive, dampening, holding back. If one learns to accept movement, all movement, then the movement becomes your master, your friend. Then one can stop trying to hold it in and to stop it. The bow will shoot itself, just as the horse will accept you and let you ride it.

'In life you must learn about movement. Never fear movement, but in essence recognise that you are movement yourself. Take down the barriers,' the master advised.

Later that afternoon, as some kind of reward for me, he asked me to stay after the young men left. He said he wanted to talk. This was his way of letting me ask questions. We walked around the small farm. We passed the irregular bonsai. He told me they had been his wife's and that after she died he could not bear to get rid of them. But neither could he be bothered with all the work that went into them. So as more time passed they became an odd memorial, clearly marking the point when she left and stopped their training.

We went back to his little tea-house near the stable. I wanted to return to my dilemma of riding in competitions and riding outside their sphere. So I started by asking him why he thought I might like to practise more than perform. At first he seemed a little incredulous because it was clear to him that practice was performance. I think he wanted me to explain how I saw them as being different. I said, 'Sometimes I feel uncertain about it. Do you think that I have some subconscious fear of competition?' I didn't honestly feel that that was the case. I can take competitions or leave them. They never meant very much to me. In my culture, if you avoid competitions, people will suggest that you are afraid of them.

He told me he thought that was unfortunate. For one thing, we are always in a competition of sorts. It is the nature of staying alive, as predators in this world of nature. Those who divorce games from life and imbue into them disproportionate importance are paradoxically escaping from the real competition of life. He felt it also unfortunate that I had been made to feel that practice was something less than so-called performances. In Japan practice is celebrated, and practice is believed to be everything. It is lifelong and always changing, but it is also constant since it seems difficult to achieve perfection.

He smiled at me. I wanted to know how practice was going to help me if I didn't prove something with it – if I didn't show someone something. He said that I had to show myself, and that anyone watching, if they wanted to see it, would. He said that practice is unlike work and also unlike play. The right practice will automatically improve one's performance at whatever is one's particular meditation. But this is not the goal. He said that you have to find out what practice can do, and why you want to practise this thing. But you must be careful not to get stuck in practice either. One must not, for instance, only

[93]

practice alone and only in perfect circumstances. That can be as much a trap as an escape.

A man is not born enlightened. Each of us is born by chance into our individual predicament. The art of living is to work through whatever might be missing in one's balance and development. The right practice at riding very quickly places one face to face with one's own inadequacies. Maybe at first one would feel it is just the body's limitations, like one's arms are short, legs too fat. Soon one goes deeper, and character and mental limitations come into play. Maybe the person has a temper, maybe the person is lazy, too feminine, or too masculine. Every day in practice one gets a concentrated dose, a chance, a time to see these problems and to work on them without the distractions of life, like going to the market, or feeding the dog. Then the person has a rest so he can come back again and again. Every day practice measures the person, and only that person can tell if he is making progress. People can fool everyone but themselves.

The world today pulls us in all directions – materialism, greed, ambition, desires, and pleasures. It is hard to restore or develop balance. In the deep meditations of the right practice, a person will be revealed to himself and given a chance to balance himself. The person will develop. The person becomes a better craftsman. This automatically happens. It is an outcome, yet it is not the reason to practise. That is what is meant by not trying to hit the target. The way you shoot is more important than what you hit. If you learn a way to shoot or a way to ride, you might find a way to live.

Inevitably, in any practice paradoxes occur – dualisms, dichotomies. They can seem irreconcilable and in fact will be irreconcilable. Logic will not yield a satisfactory answer. If you cannot find a way to handle these apparent road blocks, you will be stopped. The right practice gives one repetitive opportunities to learn to handle paradox, to train one's creativity to solve these unsolvable problems. Most people do not want to work that hard day after day. It is a shame because the rewards are great, but they are not the rewards bestowed on you from the outside. Enlightenment is not a prize. As long as you still feel a thrill when you hit the bull's eye or feel dejected by not doing so, you are still looking for external validation. You are not satisfied with who you are. In fact, you may not know who you are. You have to know from inside. You need more work on yourself. Most people just give up. They accept a certain level of performance from themselves. 'That is, after all, who I must really be'... 'I am a thief'... 'I am weak-willed'... 'I can't do that'... 'I've always been this way.' They resign themselves. Resignation is very different from acceptance.

Acceptance may be the honest admission of something, like a shortcoming or flaw. Resignation is acceptance of something plus the feeling of not being able to change that something. In the right practice one year from now you will be able to do things you could not physically or psychologically do at this moment. One must learn all one's weaknesses better than anyone else and then one must develop. One must participate in life.

The person and his horse become a team. Each affects the other. If this were not true, a person could sit on a horse and it would take you wherever it wanted to go. Life would live the person. That's really the choice, isn't it?

It was late. There were a few embers in the dark tea-house. It was time to leave. My luck had not run out. I had found another great teacher.

* * * * *

I had found a place to stay in the small city where my friend was teaching. In the first week I bought a small black and chrome motorcycle. It was almost an hour's ride one way on the little bike, but it cost almost nothing to operate. I began to like the routine of the journey, and no matter what the weather, I made the trip six days a week on my little steel horse. When the weather was fine and in the spring when the flowering cherry trees were in bloom, the ride was nothing less than a sightseeing tour. In my time off I visited museums and martial arts *dojos.* I became fascinated with simple equipment of the Samurai and the unique philosophies of honour. I saw exquisite costumes, foreboding iron masks, and the lightest silken fabrics. Swords and bows, weapons of ferocity often sublimely decorated. Once uncovered, I seemed to see this fighting spirit everywhere and I certainly felt a sense of warfare in myself.

Above all, there were the teachers of martial arts. They were calm but latently ferocious, some with technical wizardry, others with incredible strength. I would be lying if I said I was not comfortable, even pleased, with this potential violence and power. I tried to carefully observe every technique I saw. I know attacks were on my mind a lot. If you have to defend yourself, you should know how to do it well.

When I travelled to the different martial arts training centres, and even when I talked with religious people about the study of Zen Buddhism, the word 'hara' would come up again and again. I felt comfortable with this concept but needed to know more. When my chance to ask questions of the Sensei came up, I knew I had to get him to tell me more about 'hara' and 'tanden', and man's centre. The next time he asked if I had any questions, I was ready.

'Can you tell me about hara?'

'I have to laugh because sooner or later every horseman wants to know about hara, the ocean of energy. I will tell you my own experience because you are a rider so you will appreciate it. Hara is a very big concept in the East. It refers to the area below the navel. It is a three-dimensional space. In the West it is referred to as the centre of gravity, but it is much more than that. In the area is a plexus of nerves, the centre of a human being. It is a well-spring for 'ki', the energy of life. Learning to strengthen it and control it and it can send energy to all the extremities. You have seen acupuncture work its healing by unblocking nerve meridians and thus letting energy flow back into an injured area. Well, you might think of it that way.

'If you participate in martial arts or religious meditation you will be taught early on about centring in the hara, or building a strong 'koshi' (abdomen) Some of the very first and most important lessons you will receive are about breathing, learning to breathe from the abdomen, regularly and carefully. This breathing promotes relaxation. Everyone knows that no physical or mental activity of a high order can exist in strangling tension. Breathing becomes very important to settle the mind and body. In our case it is also useful to train someone to locate the tanden, the central point of the hara. At the end of an exhalation, there will be a perceptible tensing of the tanden. One of my teachers had us lie down on our backs and, with the legs straight out, lift them off the floor. At the same time we had to raise our heads up. When we found the place of greatest tension in the lower abdomen, we had found the tanden.'

'Why is there all this training to develop this area and be conscious of it? I asked him.

'For one overpowering reason: to protect oneself from the debilitating effects of gravity. Man, like the insect, is sectional with weakness in the 'hinges'. In the ant, the weak points are between the thorax and the head and between the thorax and the tail section. For man, they are in the neck, and between the thorax and the lower cavity – the koshi and hara. If care is not taken to make these areas straight and strong, gravity will cause man to collapse there. People either lean backwards, hollowing their lower backs, or slouch forward, collapsing over their stomachs, thus letting the head fall or tip without carrying balancing strength into the back. In the correct posture, the upper body is relaxed. The koshi is strong; the legs are set slightly apart under the koshi so that a plumb line from the head goes through the hara into the ground between the feet. The force of gravity is stabilised. If the legs are out in front too far, the person is pulled backward by gravity. On the ground, he would fall over backward. In riding, he is held up by the back of the horse. As you know, this is ugly and we both feel this is unethical. Our friend is overburdened, and he is also trying to be in balance.

'Anyway, I was having these breathing and meditation lessons: shoulders down and relaxed, chin slightly in, centre in the hara, letting my legs feel as if they were growing into the earth. Remember, I was being taught in the village, but I was always thinking of my horse, and I admit I was not the best student. I had heard stories of Jobajutsu, the martial art of horsemanship, of shooting a bow from a horse. But there were no horsemanship teachers. So I was always trying to apply this to riding. My teacher used to say "Posture is enough", and over and over "Posture is everything". I wanted to use ki and the forces of the hara for riding, and I experimented. I used to think, "What good is all this sitting in the meditation hall when I could be sitting on a horse? What good was it to learn posture in a vacuum?" I wanted to ride, to move. At least in other martial arts schools, they used ki and koshi (a strength-filled centre) in motion or tanden exercises for control, as in archery. But my teacher was a stickler for posture and kept coming back to "posture is everything".

'At home I was trying to shoot a bow from a running horse. I thought even the Kyudo (archery) teachers couldn't help me because they are all stood so still. I kept at it: extend the pelvis, push the neck to the back of the shirt, knees downward, do not break at the waist, be strong in the abdomen and back. In time I could steer the galloping horse by the projection of ki through the hara, leaving my hands free. It was funny because after a while I would go back to my teacher and almost argue. I don't know why the teacher tolerated me. I was a disrespectful student. I told him what I was doing as if I had finally found a practical use for all his breathing exercises and posture training. I discoursed on ki and its projection. I was an expert. Basically I told him I thought the study of posture without a use was pointless. He was very patient.

'He knew nothing of riding, but one day he asked me if, when I rode, did I have a good position or bad, and did I know if the position was off. I looked at him as if I were further going to prove my point. Of course, without good sitting you cannot ride well. Then I said that posture is everything. We both stopped cold, and he began to laugh. There I was quoting him verbatim. I had gone right around the circle. In that instant I realised what he had been trying to show me all along. Perhaps I am a little dumb and I needed the bigger feelings and motion of riding to teach me the subtle effects in a meditation hall, which I eventually saw were the same.

'This is what I saw in your riding. Someone taught you this way. I could see it in your free hands and deep seat. I realised we were oddly like opposites. I had been raised here among the masters of correct sitting, and should have learned the subtleties of correct sitting. But I had forsaken them, and went to find practical, mundane uses for this skill. But then I realised how practical the subtleties or sitting correctly are. You had controlled breathing, a deep centre, soft shoulders, and obvious control of the hara. But all your ki was just lying dormant. I couldn't believe you didn't realise how much more you could use it. That is why I had you work with my students. Your teaching on sitting was, in a sense, purer than mine because I thought you had no ulterior motives in using your hara. I didn't realise you didn't really know how to do it. So that is why I say it is funny that now you are asking me this. Maybe you are just as greedy as I was.' We both laughed.

'You have to learn to use these forces, but never for ambition or for showing off; but out of respect for nature and our friends, the horses. Balance is ethical. I think in some ways my own teacher did not give me enough credit. I was never going to use this force against nature or the horse or another man. I just wanted to ride the horse better. So I will trust you, and I will tell you all I know. Then you will have to practise for years, and become your own guide as to how you use it, and how far you will go with it.

'The projection of ki is like an awareness to the finest edges of balance – both to receive something, feel something coming toward you, and to issue something, to send a feeling away to someone or something else. I believe it is a very big force, very dramatic. But it took me years to get past this showing off, overdoing it in riding.

'The secret is this: when a horse is in motion and balance, then, as in all things in balance, very little force or weight is needed to tip the scales in one direction or another. Centre yourself in your tanden, but then try to develop a feel for light forces, just enough to guide the purposely unbalanced horse. Your shoulders stay relaxed while your upper body is open and your koshi (centre) is strong. Your legs form a firm base for slight movement or projection of your hara and ki, and send the horse in any direction. For example, in a turn, you don't throw all your weight over to one side of the moving horse. Even if it worked, it would be too upsetting. One finds the balance of the horse quickly, then slight projection of the hips and hara or a steadying. Whatever – the range is infinite. Just remember, no matter what weight is on each side of a scale, if they are in balance a feather will tip the scales.

'The biggest tip I can give you is: do not make hara into a big force. This is unnecessary and can have a reverse effect by desensitising you to subtle shifts. This is what my posture teacher kept trying to tell me. Make hara a small, subtle effect in riding, but make it constant. Concentrate low down in the abdomen and start trying to feel, and then adjust the horse from there first. The horse will let itself be trained if you are in position. Horse and rider start listening carefully to each other. Of course, all these are just words. We need to try this on the horse. That is the only real test and real knowledge.'

The more time I spent with him, the more I came to see how masterful he was at designing action-teaching situations. He disliked explanation with words, although I felt he was very good at it. I know he liked it better when he could orchestrate an incident for the student to feel, or if he himself could act out some drama. His little theatres were always effective. You could not forget the lesson when it came in these forms. I remember once he wanted to get across the importance of the rider's legs as a base of support. The horseman's seat must resemble a stance, the same in any other martial art, or for that matter in any balanced movement. It is a fact that in many martial arts, there is a horseman's stance. He didn't want to encourage a stiffening grip, but the leg contact has to be strong and secure to provide stability for the hips and the hara. If there is a weak hinge at the abdomen, just as much care must be taken to firm the bottom of the hinge, the legs, as the top of the hinge, the koshi and the back. If one side of a hinge is firm but the other is not, the joint will still fold in the middle.

There were always further instructions about not hurting the horse's back with what he called 'unethical sitting'. One day he was trying to show all of us, but especially one of the young men, that projection of ki from the hara was impossible without a good stance or seat. There was a heavy, tall stable door at one end of the building where he kept his horse. He asked us one by one to please go and push the door open. He had earlier greased the smooth floor in front of the door, and of course, as anyone pushed on the door, their feet slid away. The harder one attacked the door, the faster the attacker's feet would slide out and the harder he landed when he fell. We all ended up laughing, but the point was well made. Without any grip or friction on the floor, there was no possibility for leverage. Any force exerted forward with the hands and upper body pushing was immediately cancelled out by a backward force exerted at the feet or lower body. Whenever he saw the rider's legs sliding around backward or forward, he would remind them of the lesson of the slippery floor. Guidance would be impossible until the rider had a secure base and that base went down through the legs around the horse, and was not just on top.

I tried to learn to think more like he did, not always in idealised abstractions but through analogous, physical problems that would resonate with the issue or dilemma, thus showing a different perspective.

One day I was flabbergasted when he told me he liked

the paintings of Cezanne. Cezanne, he felt, had no trouble seeing from several perspectives at once. He told me that he preferred to teach with direct actions. It was very hard for him to entertain or present different perspectives simultaneously, with words. One looked at a painting and it was all there in front of you at one. He said it might be different for me, it was just his own preference. Oddly, over time I came to appreciate my Sensei's words more than anything else. It was his wise counsel that I went back for over and over again. He was not without frustrations, but he kept setting up his students to face their own demons. He didn't necessarily send you out alone. You always felt he had one eye on you in case you started drowning, but he would let you go under quite a few times. He had a way of giving his students a warning or a piece of advice, a weapon, so when you were in the midst of a battle you didn't feel completely out-matched.

* * * * *

In many Eastern teaching disciplines there are formal and informal opportunities for the student to ask questions of the master. It's not easy, though, to formulate an important question for your next session. Sometimes you forget what it is you want to ask, or when the time comes to put your question you get shy. You think your question is too trivial, or maybe you feel you should be able to work it out yourself. Like everyone else, it took me a very long time to learn how to formulate respectful and serious questions, and then not be afraid to bring them up when the time came.

As I continued to train with Sensei and study martial arts, I kept having a feeling that I was going to have to use them in some way and this bothered me quite a bit. Finally I went to my master and told him I had been perturbed by something from the day I arrived. I tried to explain that although I wanted to participate in the sport aspects of riding, they were increasingly in direct conflict with the art aspects. It seemed that the business of riding was getting darker and darker. Inhumanities and lack of compassion were becoming more and more common. Some popular public figures had stopped even trying to make excuses for their abusive riding, thereby almost suggesting that extensive and constant force was necessary. Others in national positions of power as teachers and judges were leading completely duplicitous lives, espousing classical principles at conventions, meetings, lectures, while running nothing short of torture chambers at their personal stables, hidden from the public eye.

On two occasions in a five-year period I arrived at two different international trainers' stables to find a tarpaulin covering a horse lying in the school, killed in a so-called riding accident. Also, I rode a horse trained by a famous woman Olympic trainer and found that the unfortunate horse would urinate uncontrollably when asked to piaffe because he had been so terrorised by the trainer's methods. Since these people were in, as I said, positions of power, the press would do nothing but glorify them.

I began thinking of these people as my enemies. My dilemma began to consume more and more of my energy. Finding ways to answer people who would say, 'Don't you think so and so is a marvellous trainer? took a tremendous amount of strength, so I ended up being silent.

The longer I was in the horse business, the more secrets I knew. The more people I met, the more direct experience I had, not just with isolated mistakes of passionate people, but long-term deliberate systematic abuse and destruction of beautiful animals. I was wanting to fight more and more. I was certain that my training had prepared me for this confrontation. I thought I had been mysteriously groomed to be a fighter worthy of these adversaries. Was my antagonism stirring because in some way I was about to go into battle? How was I supposed to fight? What was supposed to be my part in this struggle?

This was the turmoil I was in. He listened to me very carefully. In fact, the intensity with which he was listening alarmed me. I felt I had to tell him everything. When I stopped, there was a long silence before he started speaking.

'Whenever you have strong reactions that want to turn themselves into stronger actions, you must look deep into yourself. You have to be sure your reactions are not overly sensitised. There is something of a mirror in front of you. To take on the coat of a moral authority is to wear a very heavy garment. This may be your path, but it is a very difficult one.

'Know that once such a choice is made you can never indulge in indiscretions. Everything would have to stay in control. There would be no room for any decadent joy. No matter what injustice might befall you, your rage would have to be contained – no retribution comes from a passionate saint. The life of a saint is lived in a very thick bottle.

'If you choose this life, or it chooses you and you do in fact live it, I myself would bow down before you. You would deserve my respect and admiration, and you would get it. For me, it is hard enough to be an ordinary man. If, however, you fail to live as you preach, then how could I treat that hypocrisy any differently from the hypocrisy of your false horsemen? Even if you decide to step back from the life of a saint, but wish to hold on to your moral authority, there are still strategic problems that come from being a judge or a policeman. You can find yourself in the position of answering rumours, lies, or challenges of your authority. Once you incite a battle, it can become necessary to back it up, to answer every charge against you, your laws and your ideals. Answer every blow with a fiercer one from yourself. It is easy to find yourself in a reactionary place. You can lose your own direction by chasing every true and false scent of your adversaries.

'There is a real truth that no injustice, once committed, can be rectified. No one can take back the pain someone forces on another human or animal. You can get revenge to soothe your own anger, but you cannot go back in time and change what has happened. All your attention must be on the here and now. That is the only way to prevent injustice. Stay in front of it by attending to your own life. Train yourself hard so you will never be a victim or victimise others.

'I want to tell you a little story,' he said. 'There were two very great sword-makers in the time of the Samurai. A man named Maruyama was an apprentice to a legendary sword-maker named Masamune. In time, Maruyama learned everything that Masamune could teach him. His blades were some of the finest any Samurai had ever seen. As you can well imagine, they were highly prized in that time of such violence.

'Maruyama was in great demand. It was said that his blades were so sharp and kept such an edge that to test them swordsmen would take them down to a stream and stand the blade in the water. The edge was so deadly that if a leaf floated gently downstream and ran into it, the leaf would be divided without the slightest friction or hesitation. It was an awful weapon and men feared it. As good as Maruyama was, it was his teacher, Masamune, whose blades went even beyond Maruyama's – almost to divine status. When a swordsman took a Masamune blade down to the stream, it had attained such perfection that leaves floated around it. None would even come near its edge. Masamune blades went beyond destruction.

'I know that your skill,' he said finally to me, 'is now quite formidable, and yet you are nowhere close to being finished. I have no doubt that if you want to do battle, your adversaries will know it. Maybe for you, though, there is something more – more like the difference between Maruyama and Masamune.'

He stopped for a second and looked gently into my eyes. 'You notice I said Maruyama learned everything Masamune could teach him. The last thing Maruyama had to learn by himself, he did not.'

Two weeks after that meeting, Sensei died. He never let on how sick he was. He made excuses for himself on difficult days. At the end he told me with a slight smile that he had much work to do. After all, he had to help get my life in order. I promised him I would never stop trying.

I never went back to the East again.

CHAPTER SEVEN

THE DIRECTIVES
Pennsylvania, 1996

I was returning home on a flight from Europe. Continuing my efforts to complete the philosophical and physical structure of my own riding school, I had visited another well-known riding establishment. I began thinking about an odd thing. Why do so many riding instructors yell at their students?

There are excuses and explanations for this phenomenon. One is that riding is often taught in large buildings or open spaces. The riding instructor must project his or her own voice over long distances and inside some of the poorest acoustical settings. The instructor gets comfortable with shouting. This is an excuse, because what I am talking about is not really a matter of volume. Riders do not complain when their instructor is praising them at the top of their lungs. On the other hand, if the instructor whispers criticism that is vindictive or mean, even if it is constructive but strikes a sensitive spot, the reaction of the student can be that he or she is wounded. I think this emotional change is often brought about by frustration. Sometimes the instructor becomes frustrated by a student's inability to do something for a million of the right or wrong reasons. Sometimes the teacher becomes frustrated by his own inability to make himself understood or the task understandable: 'Don't ask why. Do it because I say so,' is the oft-heard motto of this kind of instruction.

In all fairness to instructors, there are times during the course of learning difficult activities when elements of danger creep in. In such circumstances an instructor may not have time for long explanations. A situation can be so urgent that the elegance of the wording used is irrelevant. If a person is about to step in front of a moving truck, you use any and all the powers of your voice to stop that person dead in his or her tracks.

There is here, though, an enormous responsibility on the part of the instructor not to squander or abuse the student's trust. When the situation merits it, lapses in protocol or manners can be forgiven. If these power-voice situations are used too routinely, they become so inflated in value that they become meaningless to the student. The instructor will lose respect. If the instructor is too regularly frustrated by a student's inabilities, both the student and the teacher have to rethink their work. Teaching is almost entirely about inabilities to do something – that is why the instructor is being sought. In spite of all these explanations, I think we are still talking about excuses for lapses in patience.

There is another case when an instructor will emotion-ally escalate a situation in order to provide more energy, either his own or the student's, or both, in order to overcome a thorny problem. There is an explanation for this on an elementary, physical level. Inside molecules at the atomic level we can find electrons revolving in an orbit of sorts around the nucleus of an atom. An electron is considered to be at its ground state when it is at its lowest energy level closest to the nucleus of an atom. This is not the only state possible for the electron because it is possible to excite the electron. When that happens it will move into a different orbit. It will change its course, in a sense. In order to do this, it needs a catalyst – more energy. Kinetic energy, heat, for example, can cause this effect.

If a riding instructor can find a digestible kind of energy to infuse into a situation or a student, the orbit of the work can be escalated to a higher level. Maybe this occurs over an impasse in the work. Unless a student has been thoroughly prepared, aimed and schooled, success from escalating a situation will be pure chance. It is probably not worth the risk. Let me give you an example. Suppose you place a person unfamiliar and untrained in computers in front of a complicated set of keyboards which run a powerful industrial task. The person is reluctant to act and will hold still in ground state. You decide to add heat as an additional energy source, and the situation hots up emotionally. Then the person starts pressing buttons and throwing switches at random. The person moves to a new level of action, but is acting without reason and is more likely to wreck the machine or cause a lot of damage than to have a desired positive effect. It would be pure chance that the person would execute the task correctly and with success. The odds of a productive outcome would be very low indeed.

If the student is prepared and trained and an escalation comes about, it can galvanise the situation and provide an impetus to move the practice to a higher level. One of the best examples of this kind of teaching can be found today in some of the more formal teachings of Zen Buddhism, in particular during 'sesshin'. Within the normal day-to-day education of the Zen Buddhist student, there are special times set aside during the course of the year for intense retreats. These might last for a week. The student lives at the Zendo which is the practice hall, or monastery, temple, whatever you wish to call it. These Zendos are often simple places, and even if they are in dramatic places, they are always austere, uncluttered – beautifully simple. Designed to limit distraction and celebrate simplicity, they are also designed to be efficient and practical.

For the time of the sesshin, the student will keep a strict schedule with heavy meditation on their particular 'koan', a riddle of sorts. The student is to try to maintain concentration on the task twenty-four hours a day, even in sleep. Life is a strict schedule of meditating, eating, listening to the talks and all-important one-to-one meetings with the Zen Master, who will quiz and check the students on their progress.

This is no game. Serious monks have been known to meditate on a single koan for years, becoming psychologically and physically taxed to the limit before they 'solve' their koan and move on to the next step. The Master does not make it easy for the student. False interpretations are reproached. Weak effort is insulting to all who have gone before you. If a person falls asleep in the middle of meditation, they must be awakened with a slap on the back with a stick, handled by a wandering proctor. Everything is aimed at crystallising effort and pressure which will help the student reach enlightenment. Personal accounts of years and lifetimes of such work and final enlightenment are wonderful stories of human effort, perseverance, courage, strength, discipline, intuition and joy. The great Zen men of the past and present were masters at infusing energy into a situation. This will serve to train the student to find energy and with that energy they will find the former unsolvable, solvable. It is nothing short of an art form as to how a student is taught to suspend logical rational progressions, or to become comfortable with perceptual shifts, and to handle paradoxes.

I found riding theory and practice to be woven together with frustrating paradoxes. A light seat is a strong and deep seat. Impulsion is and is not speed. These are some of the reasons why I have always been drawn to Zen, and Zen was my first real relief from all the dualisms, unsolvable problems and frustrations. It seemed that I could not grasp these perplexities with standard Western Cartesian thought-processes. I wanted my students to be familiar with Zen and I knew, with it, they would be able to find relief when they fell into riding's inevitable traps. So I began to use it in my teaching.

Over the years I had been continually adapting and learning different systems of teaching so I could glean some of the best methods of the different schools and training systems. For anyone who wondered, this explained my interest in the martial arts. It was the physical concepts, and also the teaching styles and systems that fascinated me. How testing and gradation was and was not deliberately employed was of special interest.

Yet, I was also aware that there is a danger when one takes educational systems out of the cultural context in which they were developed. The more I studied and tried to implement and transplant these different systems the more these cultural clashes, if you will, surfaced. The horticulturist or zoologist who transplants a plant or animal species from one ecosystem to another often does so with dire consequences, usually not apparent until years later. When some exotic species is transplanted to a new area, this is not done in a vacuum. Often it is done at the expense of the native species, which then gets dispossessed. There is something aesthetically and ethically demeaning to the native plants and animals. The natural world is replete with ecological disasters that have occurred because of the blind transplantation of competing species. The delicate balances in the natural world become upset.

I was learning that if I were to build a school, I would have to do it within the native culture of wherever I was. I used to tell my students that we didn't go to work any more in three-cornered hats, but secretly I probably wished we did. I did know that these ideas had to be blended. There has always been a classic dichotomy between the new young school and the traditional old school. The young school is unencumbered by tradition. It can react quickly to changes. It can adapt and isn't harnessed by parochial bias. It can examine all schools of the world and select from all and synthesise. However, because it hasn't had the experience of long testing of theories to codify a set of important or core principles, there is a great risk that it might accept and follow charismatic or fashionable ideas and theories which might prove to be harmful over time. Schools heavy in tradition can become cumbersome in times of change, even resistant to all change. They are intent on holding on to the status quo. The protocol which can be protective becomes strangling. Instead of protecting the school, it can be used to protect the positions of the teachers within the school or the existing bureaucracy. And it does not, therefore, protect the idea of teaching.

* * * * *

A short while after I returned from that flight I was back teaching and training at my little school. I had an excellent group of students, some of whom were good instructors themselves, some competition judges, some international competitors, some were nothing short of young artists. I also had a fairly new student who had not been with me very long. She was quiet, almost timid, but she was a natural on a horse. She had beautiful elegant lines even though she was untrained. She could sit on any horse and she had real desire.

When she came to me she had already been searching to learn about riding for years, but with each instructor she had this feeling that she wasn't sure what she was looking for. My instinct was that she was not the competitor type, but that she could become a real artist with horses. I did not feel she was weak, yet people seemed always to jump to that conclusion. I knew she would be lost in the standard equestrian world, precisely because she was of that artist material. I knew there were not many places in the world where she could develop artistically in riding. She probably reminded me of myself when I was her age, so I was especially open to her.

On this particular day she asked to see me. We set up a private meeting. She was nervous. She began by quickly explaining she felt intimidated by the other students because they were special riders. She felt that she was not, and that she was going to leave. I told her this was nonsense. For me, there was no measuring stick other than a desire to learn. I was probably a little patronising. I hoped that if I gave her a little pep-talk we could settle the whole matter, but it was not going to be that easy. She was made of stronger stuff. She told me that I didn't know how imposing I was.

I was reminded of a story an old writer friend told me. A very famous woman poet was giving a reading at an equally famous women's college which my friend attended. Just before the reading, some students were asking the poet questions and discussing their work. One hopeful young woman asked the poet if she thought that the work she was showing her would ever really be poetry. The older woman shot back a definite No! The younger woman was crushed. The poet then dismissed the lot of them and they slunk back to their seats.

The poet began the reading. When she had finished she put her papers aside and talked directly to the group, and in particular to the crushed young woman. She told the whole class what had happened. Then she stopped and looked each person in the audience in the eyes, and said sternly, 'If you cannot make it through the first "no!", then you will never be a poet.' She went on with the reading. Each person in the audience felt they had learned something very important.

So I was about to counter my student's statement very sharply with my most imposing voice, and give my own rendition of the poet's 'no' story. However, something else happened. I don't know if it was because I was exhausted from all the travelling or if something else was involved, but I felt I just couldn't come up with one more psychological ploy. I was tired of listening to others. I was tired of waltzing around sensitive personalities. I was tired of all the diplomatic patiences one must have to teach. I couldn't be aggressive, and I couldn't be soothing. I couldn't patronise nor scold. I felt I didn't want to preach, or push the plan. I didn't want to invite her to leave. I think I didn't want to do anything for her at the moment. Instead, I wanted to do something for me. For myself.

'Imposing,' I said at last, 'of course I had to try to be imposing. Do you have any idea of the opponents I have to face each day? People of fabulous wealth and power all bent on the gratification of their egos. The horses be damned. I have a very dull sword to fight with. Competitors, in some cases the people I actually compete in riding against, and top administrators routinely drug their horses to accomplish what they can't do with skill or hard work. Many use drugs themselves. Judges can judge fairly only until someone they know or have heard of enters the ring. Then no matter what happens in the sand, the score is fixed. Their minds go out of control. They have principles like feathers. At forums where they train each other, the people in power crush dissent like a bad government. They will not go outside their clique to learn anything new.

'The actions of the people in dressage are making a mockery of the great art that I love. I have had to do battle in any way that I could, although I have never underestimated my opponents. I was a realist and often saw my struggle as pathetic as Quixote's, laughable. But like Quixote I could be valiant. So I wanted to try to make my students brave and courageous, but each one had to realise the odds against us. You were going to have to do it for other reasons than actually trying to change anything. Huge corporations were investing large amounts of money in the sport of dressage. Their chosen competitors were their labels, their trademarks. They dominated the press. If you went against them, you had to be prepared for all kinds of fall-out.

'This is not your problem right now,' I told her. 'This is my problem, but someday it might also be yours. You will have to decide.'

My speech ended. It gushed out and it ended. We stood, each disarmed by our own honesty. Silent. I felt I couldn't go any further at the moment. I needed time to think. To think about myself, my school, and if there was merit to her remarks. And if there was, could I do anything about it? I asked her if she would hold off making her final decision for a couple of days. She agreed.

In the days that followed I began to meditate seriously on every aspect of my teaching. My ideas of the school's curriculum, its directives, direction, and its goals. I saw what I was doing in the establishment of my own structures, psychological and physical, as ways to legitimise and formalise my ways of teaching. I envied the great schools of the world, and I knew I was not part of them. I think I needed to make my own. I was not a fool, though, trying to make something to appease my sense of prestige or glory.

No, behind it all was still my child-like excitement of animals, and the fundamental love of horses. I felt a need to repay them. To be useful to them. I felt I needed an authoritative voice. I did not feel I could speak for them, but in a sense I knew what they wanted to say. I meant to be supportive to them, just as you would to a friend. I knew there were great historical examples for what I was trying to do. The great Guerinière was always in poor financial straits mainly because he was on the outside of the popular cliques. There was also La Broue, Newcastle ... the list went on and on, a catalogue of men dying penniless but holding on to their principles. That was the attitude that inspired me.

The next day I gave the young woman a light lesson. I stayed away from contentious points. I let her do the exercises she would be good at. It was safe teaching if it was teaching at all. But I felt I had to stay between her and her learning. It was the kind of teaching I hate.

So I went back to my ideas. I had run into a very old problem: my need to legitimise my teaching by forming a system, a construction, for my school. All of this was really a societal demand. These cultural standards were deeply embedded in me. Partially they had been placed there by a powerful society, partially kept there by my own agreement. These requirements tended to suppress the free-wheeling aspects of my teaching. This kind of teaching did not fit well in the notions of what happens in a good school. On the other hand, there were individuals with standards and requirements who had no rules and who would do anything to get the job done. This is the place where individual creativity lived. This is the place where I could teach anyway I felt I needed to. This, of course, was the reason for so long that I had had mixed feelings about that lesson with my handicapped friend many years ago. There was a long history of my suppressing my impulses. I had had a tendency not to acknowledge them as worthwhile or important. I felt they had no weight. Now I had to learn to balance the two. What an odd situation I found myself in. Was I perhaps at a crystallising moment after years of foment? And what is the catalyst? Not some great indomitable horse, nor some powerful cultural organisation snarling before me, trying to finish me off. No, this moment was crystallised by a diminutive girl-woman who I hardly knew.

On the third day we worked again. The lesson was the same, but I told her I thought I was getting to something important, and we would have to talk.

Things were becoming clearer in my mind. If my school was to be a cultural structure, she was not going to fit in my construction. It looked like I had no choice. Either I had to let her go, or let my system go. Yet, although I had built this system, no one could force me to hold it together. In my admiration of the great schools of the world, I had lost sight of the fact that the Spanish Riding School was a great school because of the great teachers, both horses and men. If they had to move out of the magnificent cultural building in the heart of Vienna, it would still be a great school. The teacher is always the bridge between a student and what is to be learned, not a school or a society. Individual teachers must reach individual students. No matter what cultural laws are imposed, what societal restraints are expressed, this is the way. The curriculum of schools cannot be transmitted without the consent of teachers. Teachers must take the credit or the blame. I began to see the school as a construct of society, to inculcate its laws and restrictions. I saw the teacher and his or her students as representing the individual's pursuit of his or her own path, his or her own freedom. I knew I would have to be the one who must adapt.

So on the third day, I told her it was important to me that I find a way to teach her. I didn't really know how, but I felt certain she would show me. She would have to teach me how to teach her. If what she wanted to know was equally as important as what I wanted to teach, we should be able to work something out. She looked a little unsure but said she very much wanted to learn. I told her we would have to go day by day. She would have to be honest with me if something began to upset her. I would try on my part to be as clear as possible, and patient. If she would talk, I would listen. Above all, we would have to communicate to hear each other, and we would have to learn to invent a way, a new system. It would be one more system in the many.

In the following days I did not feel my school dissolve. Instead I felt an odd and different kind of legitimising. I allowed the creativity which I never could stop anyway, a more acceptable place. I tore down some of my own rules. I didn't start teaching everyone differently. I think I realised I was already doing that to an extent. I was free inside a form, for to teach a discipline to a hundred people, the teacher teaches in a hundred different ways. I honestly did not know where this was leading. The only thing that was clear was that teaching could not be mass-produced. To learn something, the student had to have a teacher.

* * * * *

One evening, not long after this situation, it was very late and all my lessons for the day were finished. My evening ritual of dragging the indoor school to smooth the footing and prepare it for the next morning, had become quite an automatic habit after so many years. My arena is set off by itself, quite some distance from the stables. First I raked down the edges that had got banked up during the day's riding. Then I got my small tractor and dragged a harrow, which dug into the footing and turned it up, smoothing it out. I drove in a precise pattern until the whole arena was printless – all the neat linear grooves like a field ready for planting. My arena had bright lights, and they seemed even brighter when it got dark outside.

The big door through which I had to drive the tractor faced south. Once inside, the difference in the light was so dramatic that you couldn't see anything even one foot away from the doors. Though I knew there was a pond and woods, I could see nothing. It was always a large black square like a giant empty picture.

That night when I began raking the edges as I had done a thousand times, step by step, the same rhythm of the rake hitting the wooden bottom of the kick boards, the same pulling of the footing into the track the horses had created – the process was so mechanical I could look around while I was doing it. In my arena the short wall has mirrors. I found it interesting how certain occupations learn to use mirrors. Dancers, of course, practice with them daily. Hairdressers are so comfortable with them that they often talk to their client through the mirror even though they are only inches apart. They converse through their respective images on a piece of glass. In teaching riding the mirrors are practically miraculous. Once you have become familiar with the angles you become like a billiard player. From all over the riding hall you can see both sides of a horse and rider at once. You can stand behind a horse and rider and also see in front of them.

When I rake the arena at night, I go over the lessons of the day. I remember the glimpse of a certain horse's form. Sometimes I glance up at the prints of the famous engravings on the walls as I work my way around the rectangle. Whether it is cold or hot doesn't matter. It is always so peaceful when everyone is gone.

On this one warm evening I was engrossed in the task – tap, rake, tap, rake. I worked my way around to the mirrors. I thought I heard something outside. All the doors were closed except for the big door to the south. I saw nothing but the framed blackness. I continued – tap, rake, tap, rake. Again, I heard a metal jewel sound, like a bit jingling in a horse's mouth. I looked up and into the mirror and from that angle could see the entire arena. From the blackness a white horse stepped in. My immediate reaction was that my Spanish stallion had got loose. Just as instantly, I realised it was not him. This white horse was being ridden. I kept looking in the mirror. I was so startled. I stood dead still, my heart pounding. The horse was glistening silvery white under the bright lights. The bridle was heavy and ornate and had that dull gloss of gold through it and the reins. As soon as I could make out the image of the rider, I knew immediately who it was.

Almost above the beauty of the horse, and before I could see his face clearly, I saw that long sky-blue coat. There was only one like it, and it belonged to only one man.

The Grand Silence approached me. I couldn't move. The horse walked slowly with high cadenced steps. His long, thick mane bounced softly on his great arched neck. I could see the man's long dark boots. His yellowy deerskin gauntlet gloves. That fantastic coat with the sleeves folded back, showing an almost rosy hue in a shiny, satin-like fabric. Then the blue tight coat with its tails and buttons edged in gold. Finally his hat, one corner with a dark patina from being handled, and the other two trimmed in unusual braid. He walked straight into the middle of the arena. Finally I had to turn away from the mirrors and toward him. I was sure the image would disappear when I broke my gaze from the mirror. It did not. I turned to see him face to face.

He stopped. I was standing in front of the Grand Silence. All I could think about was that this was not in logic or reason, nor was it rational. But, my God, what a presence. Frankly, I was ecstatic to see him. Slowly he looked around my little school. He seemed to pause at each engraving and scrutinise it for a moment, and then his gaze would continue. He nodded his head slightly in approval. In the far corner I had a picture of him and when he got to it, he stopped and very, very quietly shook his head and laughed ever so softly.

My heart was racing. I couldn't explain this. I didn't care to. It was just amazing that he was here. There were a million things I wanted to ask, but this time it was I who was silent. Finally, he spoke: 'I see you have conquered the one and only thing that can stop a teacher.'

'Conquered?' I said. I looked at myself standing before him in all of his splendour: me on the ground with a farmer's rake in my hand, rubber gum-boots on my feet, my forehead beaded with perspiration, my gloves stained with sweat, mine and the horses'.

'I am afraid I don't feel much like a conqueror these

days,' I said. He kind of shrugged his shoulders as if to say it goes like that sometimes. He seemed so much more human to me, so much softer.

'Maitre,' I said, 'what is this one thing that can stop a teacher?'

He looked me in the eyes. 'That he cannot be taught.'

This time I laughed ever so softly.

He turned his white horse and walked toward the black square of the night sky. I stood there with all my questions. I wanted to talk to him for hours, but nothing had come out.

Just before he went through the door, I called out 'Maitre!' I wanted him to wait, let me formulate a question, say something more. He turned his horse halfway around and looked at me. I had nothing more to say and neither did he. He stepped into the dark. There was nothing but a great silence.

EPILOGUE

Very shortly after I finished this manuscript, in the autumn of 1997, and sent it to the publisher, I was helping one of my long-time students through her dressage phase at an Advanced level event. She had, at that time, several Advanced three-day horses. Although I have never really cared about winning or losing, I care a great deal about good riding and although this student, Amanda, was becoming more and more successful, it was the pursuit of good riding that was our common ground. It was not the pursuit of medals.

That particular Friday morning, I was at an event to help her with a brilliant but difficult white horse. This same horse was to leave for Germany in the following week to compete at Achselswang. After the Friday morning dressage phase I had to leave immediately for the airport to teach a clinic in another state. The following afternoon I received a call from my wife, who was competing in the same division as Amanda. She told me Amanda had suffered a freakish but serious fall with another of her horses, and had been rushed to the hospital in a coma.

In the subsequent months she never regained consciousness. Before she passed away, and especially in those last agonising days, I witnessed unbelievable love and heroism from her family and friends. I was asked to deliver a eulogy at her memorial service, which was one of the most difficult things I have ever had to do in my life. I had time to reflect, and I used as a theme the fact that I felt I had learned more from her than I had ever taught her. When I delivered the eulogy, I talked about her final and most compelling lesson.

The teacher is not supposed to out-live the student. When this happens, the teacher has nothing to do. What she showed me was that one's studentship is never over. As a teacher you must continue. You can never hand over the job of learning. You can never give it up and let someone do it for you. She forced me to reconnect myself to learning, to understand that there is no end. I said I thought a passionate life is hard to be around. Not because you can't stand that person's idiosyncrasies, but because they force you to stand on your own feet, to have your own life. You have to become an equal around them. You have to develop your own passion or you won't survive their flame, or their loss if they leave. They do not make you watch them as they attack life. They don't force you to be a part of their risks. But you want to watch them, as painful as it is sometimes. Why? Because they inspire you in the way they experience their life to the fullest.

In the end Amanda's and my last work together revolved around a white horse. The Grand Silence had a white horse. We all must have a white horse. The white horse is a passion. It is light.